Why Half of Teachers Leave the Classroom

Understanding Recruitment and Retention in Today's Schools

Carol R. Rinke

ROWMAN & LITTLEFIELD EDUCATION
A division of
ROWMAN & LITTLEFIELD
Lanham • Boulder • New York • Toronto • Plymouth, UK

Published by Rowman & Littlefield Education
A division of Rowman & Littlefield
4501 Forbes Boulevard, Suite 200, Lanham, Maryland 20706
www.rowman.com

10 Thornbury Road, Plymouth PL6 7PP, United Kingdom

British Library Cataloguing in Publication Information Available

Library of Congress Cataloging-in-Publication Data Available

ISBN 978-1-4758-0167-5 (cloth : alk. paper)
ISBN 978-1-4758-0168-2 (pbk. : alk. paper)
ISBN 978-1-4758-0169-9 (electronic)
Library of Congress Control Number: 2013957786

∞™ The paper used in this publication meets the minimum requirements of American National Standard for Information Sciences Permanence of Paper for Printed Library Materials, ANSI/NISO Z39.48-1992.

Printed in the United States of America

Contents

List of Figures

List of Tables

Foreword

Each year thousands of American public school teachers leave their classrooms and the teaching profession before they have completed five years on the job. This problem of teacher attrition, particularly acute in low-income schools and in hard-to-staff subject fields like mathematics and science, costs school districts hundreds of millions of dollars annually in recruitment and training expenses and has a serious impact on students. As one might imagine, a great deal of research and study in recent years has focused on this problem. Various remedies have been suggested and tried, but they have thus far been largely ineffective. The problem persists.

Professor Carol Rinke's book *Why Half of Teachers Leave the Classroom: Understanding Recruitment and Retention in Today's Schools* offers some important new insights on the subject that will enable the reader to better understand and appreciate the complex new dynamics of teacher career trajectories, the forces that shape them, and the implications these recent structural developments have for the teacher profession in the future.

Rinke's book, in fact, touches on a number of critical issues—beyond teacher attrition and retention—that confront education and the teaching profession today: the recruitment of teachers for hard-to-hire subjects, the initial preparation of teachers (traditional vs. shorter, alternative routes) and their continued professional development, and the day-to-day challenges of teaching in highly diverse urban schools. The relevance of this book in providing thoughtful insights on these and other important educational issues is clearly one of its strengths.

In this book, Rinke illuminates the "revolving door" of teachers' careers by seeking to "give a face to the numbers behind teacher attrition, particularly in high-need classrooms" (p. xiii). Professor Rinke offers an articulate and moving account of the early professional careers of a group of secondary science teachers from an urban school district. She situates the study in the research tradition that examines teachers' lives through their own perceptions (for example, Bullough, 1989; Goodson, 1992; Levin, 2003). Her focus on science teachers has particular relevance because theirs is a hard-to-hire field, and their high rate of early attrition presents an ongoing problem for school districts.

The core of Rinke's study lies in a longitudinal survey as well as carefully crafted case studies of eight teachers selected from the larger cohort. The case studies include six women and two men, six whites and two African Americans; and their ages ranged from the early twenties to the mid-forties at the time the study began. A high percentage of the case study teachers (six of the eight) received their professional preparation in alternative programs (e.g., Teach for America) rather than in traditional university-based programs—a phenomenon not unusual in urban school districts. Rinke categorizes the eight as *stayers* (those who stayed in the classroom), *shifters* (those who shifted within the field of education), and *leavers* (those who left education).

As is often the case with interviews and other forms of narrative research, the authentic voices of the participants emerge distinctly and powerfully. We see, for instance, vivid portrayals of neophyte teachers struggling with the day-to-day vicissitudes of teaching in highly diverse urban schools, where they often had to deal with inadequate facilities and supplies, a sometimes-less-than-supportive principal, and noncollaborative colleagues. For instance, third-year teacher Matt explained his reasoning for leaving urban teaching for a suburban district. He commented:

> I'm tired of enforcing basic rules all the time. Why do I feel so drained and feel like I'm not living life to its fullest? You know, if I was changing everybody's lives, that's different. But to go through all that punishment, it's not enough. It's not worth it. I could die tomorrow. I could die next year. This isn't living life. (p. 48)

Is it any wonder, a reader might reflect, why teachers leave the profession? All of us who care about education might ask the question: Why should teaching be so hard?

For various reasons, which Rinke delineates, the teaching profession has become far less stable than it was in the 1950s. Teachers no longer, as a matter of career choice, remain in the classroom for thirty years. Rinke uses the term *exploratory* to characterize today's environment for new teachers, with so many of these teachers coming through alternative certification programs with the intention to "explore teaching," and such a high percentage of them leaving the profession within the first five years.

But *exploratory* means something more for Rinke: It also refers to the way *all* teachers, however committed to the classroom, continue weighing their career options, often within education but sometimes beyond it. She provides examples of teachers in all three of her categories—shifters, leavers, and stayers—who engage in this exploratory practice as they actively construct their career trajectories. Clearly Rinke has identified a significant feature of the teaching profession today that must be acknowledged and reckoned with by educators concerned with filling classrooms with seasoned, competent teachers.

Rinke's book is not only an interesting personal account of the professional lives of teachers during their early years. Her study has made important contributions to the research literature on teacher development:

1. She has demonstrated that new teachers' intentions about whether they will stay in the profession "for the long haul" or for just a few years turn out to be a powerful predictor of their career trajectories.
2. Rinke has proffered a useful theoretical model to explain how teachers' career trajectories are grounded in their original plans or intentions but subsequently shaped by their ongoing experiences. She goes on to provide a close, critical examination of career trajectories as they unfold, develop, proceed—guided by initial plans but constantly modified and shaped by shifting workplace conditions, new opportunities, and personal situations.
3. She has also made a substantive contribution to the research that demonstrates the importance for teachers, especially new teachers in difficult schools, to have effective and supportive administrators (Day, Sammons, Stobart, Kington, & Gu, 2007); conversely, she shows the problems it raises for teachers to have nonsupportive and incompetent school leaders (Ladd, 2011, as cited by Rinke, 2013). No fewer than seven of the eight case study teachers reported problems with their principals. Rinke has contributed to our understanding of the vital importance of school principals by demonstrating in clear terms how they influenced the teachers' construction of their careers.
4. In this book, the author also produced the new finding that it is not only school districts and students that pay the price for early teacher attrition; early leavers themselves often face unanticipated difficulties in transitioning to new careers: for example, time and expense of further education or training, dealing with many letters of rejection, and having to accept positions below their qualifications.

In summary, *Why Half of Teachers Leave the Classroom* is an interesting and provocative book. It adds significantly to our understanding of the complex processes affecting teachers' thinking, particularly in regard to their decision to remain in the classroom, seek further employment in the broader education field, or leave education altogether. Because of its timely focus and its contents, the book has important riches to offer a variety of readers—teacher educators, graduate students in education, school district and school administrators (particularly principals), teachers themselves, and community members concerned about the issues the book so powerfully addresses. I am pleased to recommend the book to all such readers. They will, I believe, find this book as tantalizing and enlightening as I have.

Gerald J. Brunetti
Saint Mary's College of California

Preface

It is a familiar statistic: almost half of all teachers will leave the classroom within their first five years in the profession. The largest occupation in the United States has been called a "revolving door" where qualified teachers enter and, largely dissatisfied with the workplace conditions they find in schools, leave unhappy after a few short years. The situation is far worse in high-need subject areas like science and in high-poverty schools, where up to 20 percent of teachers may leave in any given year. We know the statistics, but who are the teachers? How and why do they decide to devote their expertise and passion to developing young people? And why, after investing considerable time and resources in becoming educators, do they decide to change career paths? This book is designed to give a face to the numbers behind teacher attrition, particularly in high-need classrooms. Using mixed research methods across years of early career development, *Why Half of Teachers Leave the Classroom* paints a picture of teachers who follow their hearts both into and out of the classroom.

This book aims to unpack the statistics behind the teacher workforce by taking an in-depth look at one sub-set of teachers likely to leave the classroom: beginning science teachers in a high-poverty urban school district. The book builds upon a study spanning a seven-year period, from 2005 to 2012, which followed beginning science teachers in one urban district as they developed as professionals. The goals of this study were to better understand the career paths of this particular group of educators as well as the process they went through to determine their own trajectories. Perhaps most importantly, this book aims to capture the career development of this group of teachers over time and share their experiences. While we know that 46 percent of new teachers will leave the classroom in the first five years, this book helps us to understand those teachers' unique goals, passions, skills, frustrations, rewards, and methods for constructing their own futures. In this book, we will come to know eight individuals, three who are still in the classroom in new contexts, two who have shifted to education-related positions, and three who have left education altogether. In this way, this book puts a face to one of the most vulnerable sections of America's teacher workforce.

This book also makes a case for the high cost of attrition to the teachers themselves. The negative impact of teacher attrition has already been well-documented in relation to reduced student achievement and high financial costs. This book shows that the often-young people who decide to become teachers also suffer. They invest years during a critical period of their professional lives exploring a career that they frequently choose to leave, they invest financially in training and preparation, and they invest emotionally in a career that at times leaves them frustrated and exhausted. But perhaps most importantly, those who choose to move out of education and into another field find themselves without the necessary skills to make a smooth career transition, necessitating years of re-training and interim positions before they can start over on a new professional pathway.

Finally, this book demonstrates that beginning teachers are aware very early in their time in the classroom of their intentions to remain in the field of education or use the field as a temporary stop along the way to a more lasting career path. This book offers evidence that teachers' self-reports about their own career plans have statistically significant associations with where they are professionally seven years down the road. This information, combined with what we learn about the high costs of teacher attrition, suggest the need to attend more carefully to teachers' ideas about the profession right from the start and offer greater autonomy to teachers in constructing their own career pathways.

INTRODUCING THE TEACHERS

The typical teacher in the United States is White, female, forty-three years old, and has fifteen years of teaching experience. While the typical urban teacher is somewhat younger, less experienced, and more likely to come from an ethnically or racially diverse background, overall general demographic patterns hold true across school contexts. When these teachers leave education, their attrition is usually understood as due to either personal characteristics (e.g., academic achievement, family or personal responsibilities, preparation pathway) or aspects of the workplace context (e.g., school leadership, student discipline, professional autonomy). And, apart from those who leave because of retirement or to pursue other teaching positions, by far the largest percentage of science teachers leave due to dissatisfaction with the profession.

This book follows a cohort of beginning science teachers in one urban school district as they develop their careers over a seven-year period. The chapters capture the experiences of eight teachers in greater depth, illustrating their personal and professional journeys as well as their decision-making processes as they move into new classrooms, roles, and even professions. Those who read this book—teaching candidates, teachers, teacher educators, school and district leaders, policy makers, and interested citizens—should consider where these educators are *most likely* to end up. The eight case study teachers are each introduced here as I met them at the beginning of the study. I encourage all readers to predict where they will be seven years down the road. Who is most likely to remain in an urban school? Who will switch to a more well-resourced educational context? Who will become a district or national leader in the field? And who will decide that education is not the right match, and adopt a new profession entirely? Through asking, and later answering, these questions, we come to a more nuanced understanding of teachers' career trajectories and challenge some of the long-standing assumptions about what brings teachers to the classroom and what ultimately causes them to leave.

Alexandra was a White woman who was in her early 20s at the beginning of the study. A biology and theater major at a liberal arts college, she applied directly to Teach for America upon college graduation and was placed in a large, comprehensive high school. She expressed a passion for connecting science with people and directed the school play.

Alison was a White woman in her early 20s who completed an undergraduate chemistry degree and teaching certificate before moving directly into classroom teaching. She taught chemistry at a comprehensive high school that was subsequently closed and restructured. An avid sports fan, she was often seen attending her students' games.

Charlotte was a White woman in her late 20s when she started teaching. After majoring in physics at a major technical university, she attended two years of a doctoral program in astrophysics before deciding to pursue teaching as a short-term transitional activity. She was hired at an alternative high school and enrolled in graduate education coursework.

Denise was an African American woman who herself graduated from urban public schools before majoring in biology at a Historically Black University. After rejecting medicine, pharmacy, and scientific research, Denise decided upon teaching, applied to a local alternative certification program, and taught at a large, comprehensive high school.

Matthew was a White man in his late 20s when he began teaching. His passion lay in wildlife biology, which he studied at a major technical university. After becoming disillusioned with seasonal jobs in biological fieldwork and advocacy, Matthew enrolled in a master's program for urban education and taught at a small, restructured high school.

Mitch was a White man in his late 20s who, pressured by his parents, earned a doctorate in chemistry from a prestigious private university. Upon completion, he decided to pursue his true passion for education and enrolled in Teach for America. Mitch was placed in an all-girls magnet high school where he taught both chemistry and biology.

Raya was a White woman in her mid-40s when she decided to leave a varied and successful career in science media and communications to pursue urban teaching. Calling it her "peace corps," Raya enrolled in an alternative certification program and taught at a small, restructured high school where she developed numerous community partnerships.

Tara was an African American woman in her early 30s and the mother of two children when she decided to leave a lucrative but stressful career in pharmaceutical research to achieve greater work-family balance. Herself a graduate of urban public schools as well as a private liberal arts college, Tara taught chemistry in a small, restructured high school.

WHERE ARE THEY NOW?

The following chapters answer the question, "Where are they now?" by sharing the career trajectories of these eight teachers, looking at career development across the larger cohort, and identifying themes that cut across their experiences. The introductory chapter frames the notion of teaching as exploratory in today's world by highlighting the evidence for a new workplace context. This chapter also introduces the theoretical framework, research question, and methodology. Finally, in this chapter the notion of intentions is introduced as an important theme cutting across the experiences of the beginning educators.

Chapter 2 provides an overview of the district as a whole, between 2005 and 2012, based on the survey results. In this chapter we learn more about this particular cohort of science teachers, the paths they followed into the classroom, and their professional goals and plans. This chapter demonstrates that while they stayed longer than predicted, with 63 percent teaching longer than six years, they almost universally continued along their original pathways either into or out of the field of education. We also see that professional intentions in the early years of teaching are more closely associated with later career paths than other demographic characteristics such as age, race/ethnicity, certification route, or even engagement in professional development activities.

Chapters 3, 4, and 5 capture the personal and professional journeys of the eight case study teachers over the seven-year study period. In chapter 3 we learn about the career pathways of those teachers who remained in the classroom, both in the original urban setting and in a more well-resourced suburban context. We find that these teachers discovered a way to thrive, even if it was not as they initially envisioned. Chapter 4 contains the narratives of the two teachers who shifted into education-related contexts. We see that they retained their commitment to the field of education, when their relationships with colleagues and administrators eroded. Chapter 5 illustrates the experiences of the three teachers who left the field of education altogether. In this chapter, we witness the financial, professional, and emotional challenges they endured as they found their way along new career pathways.

Chapter 6 returns to the exploratory context and compares the career paths of teachers in this context with those of teachers operating in countries that highly value educators, such as Singapore and Finland. This chapter also introduces the recruiting practices of three successful models in the United States—Central Penn High School, The Equity Project Charter School, and Aspire Public Schools—where they are closely listening to teachers' ideas about the profession. Finally, this chapter returns to the notion of intentions and suggests the importance of attending to teachers' professional ideas and plans right from the start of their careers in the classroom.

Acknowledgments

Any work of research, and longitudinal work in particular, would not be possible without multiple partnerships and supports. First and foremost, I am deeply indebted to the teachers who stayed with this research over a seven-year period, responding to my surveys and continuing to speak me year after year. Thank you in particular to the eight case study teachers who I call Denise, Matthew, Raya, Alison, Mitch, Alexandra, Charlotte, and Tara. Thank you for allowing me to follow you from school to school and workplace to workplace, always making the time to talk with me whatever the circumstances. You have contributed greatly not only through your teaching, but also by sharing your professional and personal journeys. I would also like to thank the three schools and school districts who opened up their recruitment practices as models for the field, William Grant at Central Penn High School, Zeke Vanderhoek at The Equity Project Charter School, and Heather Kirkpatrick at Aspire Public Schools.

I also would like to acknowledge the institutional supports that have allowed me to continue pursuing this research that I am so passionate about over many years: First, the Culture, Language, Literacy, and Schooling Fellowship at the University of Maryland, followed by research and professional development grants at Gettysburg College. In addition, time to research, think, write, and reflect, so critical and difficult to come by in today's world, was provided through a pre-tenure research leave from Gettysburg College. These supports made the research possible. I feel particularly fortunate to have received this assistance for often-underfunded work on teachers' lives during a time of tight budgets and limited resources for education.

Thank you also to the many mentors and colleagues who have helped to critique, support, and refine my research practice and ideas over time. Linda Valli, Bruce VanSledright, Janet Coffey, Jennifer King Rice, David Imig, and Morva McDonald at the University of Maryland provided initial guidance and critique on the first phase of this research and were particularly helpful in shaping research questions, methods, and the theoretical framework. Colleagues Gloria Park and Lynnette Mawhinney read earlier drafts of this work and have continually provided feedback as the project evolved over time and new colleague Lee Shaefer offered some wonderful insights on draft chapters. Jerry Brunetti gave careful attention to the ideas presented and their relationship to the larger field

of research. Finally, my Gettysburg and Marist College Education colleagues have provided support and a willing ear as this research took on
new forms.

Finally, I would like to thank my family – my parents Linda and Dick
Riegelman for inspiring a lifelong curiosity about career trajectories. To
my in-laws Nomi and Ronald Rinke for keeping the children entertained
while I worked on this book. To my children Coby and Noah Rinke who
have grown up with this work and are both planning fruitful careers as
scientist-artists. And of course my husband, Michael Rinke, for being my
partner in academia and in life, listening to my musings at all hours of
day and night, and making me laugh.

ONE

Teaching as an Exploratory Career

The teaching profession is anything but static, shifting along with larger workplace patterns, school reform efforts, and societal changes. While teaching has always been a vehicle of social mobility in the United States, typically attracting college-educated, middle-class professionals, other aspects of the profession have changed substantially over the past two centuries. Teaching has moved from a predominantly male to an overwhelmingly female occupation, from a largely White to a somewhat more diverse workforce that incorporates educators from a variety of racial and ethnic backgrounds, and from primarily young and inexperienced to more seasoned personnel. This last point is underscored by the historian John Rury's (1989) comments:

> Throughout most of American history, teachers have been quite young. . . . Teaching was a pursuit undertaken in one's youth, before starting the serious business of life—whether it was a career in a learned profession for men, or marriage and family for women. (p. 11)

Rury explains that it is only since the 1950s that teachers have remained in the classroom for a thirty-year career or returned to teaching after a short period of staying home to raise children. Likewise, it is only since that time that career ladders have reflected this approach.

New developments raise the question of whether the teaching profession is once again returning to its historical roots as a temporary occupation. Several factors have come together in recent years to reframe teaching as a career in the United States and other countries with similar approaches. Increased professional opportunities for women and minorities, multidimensional notions of career paths, and a proliferation of preparation routes have simultaneously impacted how new teachers view the profession, such that some beginning educators now come to the classroom with the idea of temporarily exploring teaching. While not

1

all educators take this approach, it is important to acknowledge that many educators, particularly in high-need fields, are operating within an exploratory context for teaching. This new context, which in many ways reflects the historical foundations of teaching, has important implications for how new teachers approach the profession, experience their work in classrooms, and construct their career trajectories.

This chapter first introduces the exploratory context for teaching, both its origins and implications. Then it frames the research presented in this book, which follows one cohort of beginning urban science teachers over a seven-year period, capturing their career trajectories as well as how they experience the profession within this exploratory context. Finally, this chapter presents the major findings of the research and the argument outlined in this book: that today's teachers, operating in an exploratory context, have a clear understanding of their intentions within the profession right from the start. Consequently, the field of education would be well-served to attend closely to these intentions, thereby increasing the professionalism and autonomy of educators in constructing their own career paths.

THE EXPLORATORY CONTEXT FOR TEACHING

Origins of Teaching as Exploration

In their book *Finders and Keepers*, Susan Moore Johnson and the Project on the Next Generation of Teachers (2004) frame what they term "today's teachers" (p. 19), who hold surprisingly different motivations and expectations from their predecessors just a generation earlier. Johnson and her team argue that one of the primary causes of this change is the elimination of the "hidden subsidy" for public education. The teaching workforce for years benefited from limited professional opportunities for both women and minorities, who sought out education as a means of social and economic mobility. However, in recent years the workforce as a whole has provided a wider variety of well-paying and well-respected professional opportunities, with far fewer women and minorities selecting teaching as a result.

Coupled with these changing workforce patterns is an expectation, among those currently entering the workforce, that their career paths will be far less linear and more multifaceted than in their parents' generation. This holds true not only for teachers, but for workers across sectors. Anthropologists Peter Dwyer and Johanna Wyn, in their book *Youth, Education, and Risk* (2001), draw upon their multinational longitudinal research to argue that today's young workers lead multidimensional careers that change direction over time and take into account both professional and personal factors. Many corporate and popular media accounts of the "millennials" or "Generation Y" also claim that this current generation prizes flexibility, collaboration, and making a contribution (e.g., Howe & Strauss, 2000; Walker, 2008). These larger patterns are reflected in the field of education as well (Smethem, 2007). Changing expectations of what it means to have a career also contributed to the notion that individuals may come to teaching across the life span and stay for one chapter of a longer professional journey.

The blurring of traditional lines into and out of the profession has also been facilitated by policy changes encouraging the proliferation of alternative routes into the classroom. In their review of teacher education programs, Kenneth Zeichner and Hilary Conklin (2005) note that forty-six U.S. states offer some form of alternative route into the classroom, as compared with only eight states in 1983, such that alternatively certified teachers constitute 19 percent of the teacher workforce (Papay, 2007). Research on alternative certification programs has had mixed results, generally showing no difference in quality while improving recruitment of minority teachers and teachers in high-need fields (Shen, 1998; Zeichner & Conklin, 2005). Moreover, there is a growing consensus that it is program features, rather than structure, that characterize the teacher preparation experience (Humphrey, Wechsler, & Hough, 2008).

Alternative certification has contributed to the exploratory context for teaching not only through its reduced barriers to entry that abbreviate the teacher preparation period, but also through its at-times explicit mission of preparing not classroom teachers but educational leaders. For instance, one of the most prominent and prestigious alternative pathways is Teach for America in the United States and Teach for All internationally, currently represented in twenty-six countries around the globe. These programs conceptualize their mission as developing leaders who work to solve educational inequality in multiple ways, not only through classroom teaching. For instance, the Teach for America website states:

> Teach for America is growing the movement of leaders who work to ensure that kids growing up in poverty get an excellent education. We recruit a diverse group of leaders with a record of achievement who work to expand educational opportunity, starting by teaching for two years in a low-income community. We provide intensive training, support and career development that helps these leaders increase their impact and deepen their understanding of what it takes to eliminate educational inequity. A growing movement of leaders, nearly 28,000 strong, works at every level of education, policy and other professions, to ensure that all children can receive an excellent education. (Teach for America, 2013)

Teach for America and similar programs, while pursuing the admirable goal of reducing educational inequality, also contribute to the growing sense that teaching serves as a stepping-stone to other fields.

Implications of Teaching as Exploration

This confluence of factors—increased workforce opportunities, expectations for a multidimensional career, and the proliferation of alternative pathways—has shaped what can be considered an exploratory context for many new teachers. Within this context, a series of recent international studies has investigated teachers' career pathways and identified a clear division in the teacher workforce among those who consider teaching to be a long-term profession and those who consider it a short-term occupation. A number of typologies have been developed, each with its own terminology, but with a common thread indicating that there are now subgroups of teachers with different ideas about and plans within the field of education (see table 1.1 for an overview of current typologies).

Peske, Liu, Johnson, Kauffman, and Kardos (2001), members of Harvard's Project on the Next Generation of Teachers, argued that today's teachers have short-term expectations of their time in the classroom and within that group hold either contributing or exploring orientations. Smethem (2007), working in the United Kingdom, similarly identified new teachers as career teachers, those with ambitions for promotion within the field, classroom teachers who remained committed to working with students, and portfolio teachers who viewed teaching as temporary work in building a varied career. Watt and Richardson (2008, 2012), Australian researchers working with worldwide collaborators on the FIT-Choice Project investigating factors influencing teaching choice, likewise found that among teachers there existed highly engaged persisters who planned to spend their whole careers in the classroom, highly engaged switchers who aimed for greater variety in their careers, and lower-engaged desisters who saw better career prospects in other fields. Finally, Freedman and Applebaum (2008, 2009), working specifically in urban schools, categorized teachers as traditional stayers in the classroom, leavers who were no longer teaching but remained in urban education, and leavers who left education altogether.

This emerging notion of teaching as exploratory is also reflected in increased rates of attrition from the field. Our understanding of the issues surrounding teacher retention in the United States comes primarily from the work of Richard Ingersoll and colleagues, who conducted a series of analyses on the Schools and Staffing Survey and Teacher Follow-up Survey from the National Center for Educational Statistics (e.g., Ingersoll, 1999; Ingersoll, 2001, 2003a; Ingersoll & Perda, 2011). This body of work demonstrates that beginning teacher cumulative attrition reaches 46 percent after the first five years in the classroom.

It also demonstrates that the highest proportion of those teachers, 29 percent, leave teaching because of dissatisfaction due to salary, administrative support, student discipline, and other problems (Ingersoll, 2003a). Ingersoll's work has been particularly influential in explaining how

Table 1.1.   Typologies of Teachers in an Exploratory Context

Authors	Categories
Peske, Liu, Johnson, Kauffman, & Kardos (2001)	Contributing Exploring
Smethem (2007)	Classroom Career Portfolio
Watt & Richardson (2008)	Highly Engaged Persisters Highly Engaged Switchers Lower-Engaged Desisters
Freedman & Applebaum (2008)	Traditional Stayers Leavers Remaining in Urban Education Leavers

school staffing challenges stem not from an inadequate supply of qualified teachers, but instead from elevated rates of turnover and attrition (Ingersoll, 2003b). Following Ingersoll's lead, this book differentiates between turnover, indicating movement between schools, and attrition, which suggests departure from the field of education altogether.

Recently, Ingersoll and Merrill have argued that the teaching workforce, which has traditionally been characterized by higher rates of attrition than comparable professions such as nursing, has destabilized even further (Ingersoll & Merrill, 2012). Ingersoll and Merrill show that attrition from the field of education altogether rose 41 percent between 1988 and 2008. In particular, the highest rates of attrition came from beginning teachers working in high-poverty and high-minority schools. The rate of first-year teachers leaving the field also rose 34 percent during the same twenty-year period. Ingersoll and Merrill (2012) explain:

> Not only are there far more beginners in the teaching force, but these beginners are less likely to stay in teaching. Members of the largest group within the largest occupation in the nation have been leaving at relatively high rates, and these rates have steadily increased in recent decades. (p. 17)

Their work suggests that this exploratory context is not merely conceptual, but is played out in concrete ways as teachers come into and leave the profession in high numbers.

UNDERSTANDING TEACHERS IN AN EXPLORATORY CONTEXT

The research captured in this book aims to unpack how one group of high-need teachers experienced the current exploratory context, asking the overarching research question, "How do today's urban science teachers, operating in an exploratory context, experience the teaching profession over time?" Specifically, this study utilizes mixed methods research including an initial and follow-up survey to all beginning science teachers in one urban district as well as eight longitudinal, qualitative case studies conducted over a seven-year period. Using these approaches, the research follows one cohort of teachers as they begin their careers, experience the teaching profession, and construct their professional trajectories both within and outside of education over time.

While the findings from this study have implications for the field as a whole, its particular focus on beginning science teachers in a high-poverty and majority-minority school context places it at the center of current dilemmas over teacher workforce development. We know from the work of Ingersoll and others (e.g., Ingersoll, 2003a) that beginning teachers are the most likely to leave teaching, reaching a cumulative attrition rate of 46 percent within their first five years in the classroom. While some level of teacher attrition is certainly desirable, overall these elevated rates result in high costs for schools and students. Financial estimates vary, but one study estimated the costs of teacher attrition to be as high as $7.34 billion annually across the country, and $19 million in the district under study alone (NCTAF, 2007). There is also growing evidence that teacher turnover is detrimental to students, both because teachers' effectiveness increases with experience, at least during the first few years (Grissmer, Flanagan, Kawata, & Williamson, 2000; Henry, Fortner, & Bastian, 2012), and because turnover of any kind has a disruptive effect on student achievement (Ronfeldt, Loeb, & Wyckoff, 2013).

While some of the evidence is mixed, overall there is a consensus that attrition rates are highest in high-poverty and high-minority schools, often located in urban areas. Urban schools lose approximately 20 percent of their teaching force annually, both to higher-resourced schools as well as to other professions (Ingersoll, 2003a). Ingersoll and Perda (2011) note that this is particularly true for math and science teachers, writing:

> There is a large, annual, asymmetric reshuffling of a significant portion
> of the math science teaching force, with a net loss on the part of poor,
> minority, rural and urban schools and a net gain to nonpoor, nonmi-
> nority suburban schools. (p. 588)

Because teachers of color are also more likely to work in these same urban schools, these high rates of attrition also result in a loss of diversity from the teaching force overall (Ingersoll & Merrill, 2012).

Finally, science teachers stand at the center of the nationwide struggle to construct and sustain a stable teaching force. Current popular reports (e.g., Friedman, 2005) and federal initiatives (e.g., 100Kin10, 2013; The White House, 2013) have recognized that recruiting and retaining science teachers is at the heart of efforts to enhance student achievement and raise international competitiveness. Science and mathematics classrooms are consistently difficult to staff (Ingersoll & Perda, 2011) and have the highest rates of teacher turnover, 15.6 percent and 16.4 percent respectively (Ingersoll, 2003a). In addition, science teachers in particular have significantly higher rates of dissatisfaction as compared with teachers of other subjects (Ingersoll, 2003b). These elevated rates of turnover and dissatisfaction have often been explained by the high opportunity costs for teaching and the wide variety of attractive career alternatives available in the sciences (Murnane & Olsen, 1990; Theobald & Michael, 2002).

Together, these factors point to the importance of understanding the career experiences of beginning teachers in some of the highest-need urban, science classrooms. While the unique experiences of these individual educators do not directly translate to all educators, they can shed light upon how one critically important cohort of teachers experiences the profession within the current exploratory context. The section that follows explains the theoretical model and research methods underlying this work.

A Model of Teachers' Career Trajectories

The research question is grounded in a model of career trajectories in which teachers' career paths are influenced by the interaction between their life experiences and their workplace contexts with an emphasis on the perception of success. This active and ongoing negotiation results in three possible career trajectories: continuation within classroom teaching, shifting to an education-related but nonteaching position, or attrition from the field of education altogether. Figure 1.1 outlines the theoretical underpinnings of the study, which place this process of negotiation at the center of career decision making. Moreover, this theoretical foundation emerges from an interpretivist approach to research, grounded in the meaning that individuals construct for their personal and professional lives (Denzin & Lincoln, 2011). This section highlights some of the most influential research underlying this model of teachers' career trajectories.

Life Experiences

The theoretical framework is grounded in the body of literature on teachers' lives and careers. Carter and Doyle (1996) define the field as one which incorporates both teachers' narratives as well as their career and work cycles. Perhaps the most seminal work in this field is Lortie's (1975) study on the socialization of schoolteachers, which highlights the role of teachers' rationales for entering the profession, goals, and purposes in their professional growth. Numerous studies have built upon this line of inquiry, stressing the process of learning to teach (Bullough, 1989), the experiences in teachers' professional lives (Goodson, 1992), the role of gender and race in teaching (Biklen, 1995; Foster, 1997), and the develop-

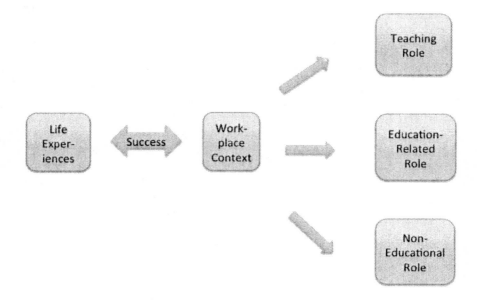

Figure 1.1.   Theoretical Model for Teacher Career Trajectories

ment of teacher pedagogy over time (Levin, 2003). Feiman-Nemser and Floden (1986) have called this body of research the cultures of teaching because it privileges teachers' own perspectives and life experiences in shaping career pathways.

Workplace Contexts

In this model, teachers' life experiences interact with their workplace contexts. Existing research highlights some of the key features of workplace context that play a role in teachers' career trajectories. For instance, influential work in this field has highlighted key features of effective schools for teacher career development, including coherent goals, teacher collaboration, and teacher learning (Rosenholtz, 1989). Related work has also emphasized the importance of salary (Imazeki, 2002), geography (Boyd, Lankford, Loeb, & Wyckoff, 2005), school facilities (Buckley, Schneider, & Shang, 2005), and administrative support (Horng, 2009) in shaping teacher satisfaction with workplace conditions. DeAngelis and Presley (2011) have noted that teacher retention decisions are largely influenced by school-level factors, indicating the importance of local workplace conditions upon teacher career paths.

The Process of Negotiation

The heart of teacher career decision making lies in the interaction between teachers' life experiences and their workplace contexts. Neither life experiences nor workplace contexts shape career pathways alone; rather, it is in the filtering of school-based experiences by life experiences that teachers perceive their own success and determine their professional futures. Previous research suggests that teachers hold a continuum of orientations toward the educational system that emerge out of their own biographies (Rinke, 2009, 2011). These orientations serve as filters to interpret and manage the rewards and challenges that regularly arise in school contexts, guiding teachers to alternately redouble efforts or shift emphasis, strengthen or adjust relationships, and even seek new jobs or change careers as a result.

Johnson and Birkeland (2003) identify the importance of a sense of success and argue that "New teachers' perceptions of whether or not they were meeting the needs of the students in their classrooms—their sense of efficacy—infused their accounts of job satisfaction and career plans" (Johnson, 2004, p. 80). Research on this interaction indicates that success can be constructed in diverse ways by teachers, including redefining traditional notions of achievement (Smulyan, 2004). It also shows that bridging the gap between teachers' visions and their context-bound practice is vital to their career development (Hammerness, 2006). Together, this body of research indicates that teachers' career trajectories are largely formed in the negotiation between their life experiences and their workplace realities, with an eye to gaining a sense of success in the profession.

Career Trajectories

This ongoing negotiation between life experiences and workplace contexts ultimately guides teachers as they construct their career trajectories. An accumulation of research indicates that rather than simply selecting between the two options of retention and attrition, today's teachers have a third option to move into non-classroom roles in the field. Termed role shifting (Quartz et al., 2008) or role differentiation (Donaldson et al., 2008), it is increasingly clear that as teachers move out of the novice years, they seek out opportunities to both grow as professionals and share their expertise with others (Margolis, 2008). This body of research suggests that as teachers negotiate their career pathways, they foresee opportunities to continue in the classroom, shift into an education-related role, or move out of the field altogether into noneducational roles.

By asking the question, "How do today's urban science teachers, operating in an exploratory context, experience the teaching profession over time?" this research aims to capture the ways in which teachers negotiate life experiences with workplace contexts, seek a sense of success, and construct meaningful career trajectories both within and outside of the classroom.

Research Background and Methods

Study Site

The research for this book was conducted between 2005 and 2012 in what will, for the sake of anonymity, be called William City, a midsize and historically industrial city on the Eastern Seaboard of the United States. William City's public school district enrolls approximately 85,000 students annually and employs over 10,000 teachers and other school-based personnel. Currently, 86 percent of students in the district are African American, 84 percent are low income as defined by eligibility for the free and reduced-price meals (FARMS) program, and 3.1 percent are English language learners. Although student achievement has traditionally been low across the district, reporting a 54 percent graduation rate and 36 percent passing rate on the major science high school exit exams at the initiation of this study, district officials have introduced a number of programs to improve academic progress, and both graduation rates and standardized test scores are on the rise. In 2011, the district boasted a 72 percent graduation rate and 55.5 percent passing rate on the science exit exam.

Over the past two decades, William City has hired hundreds of teachers each year from alternative certification programs such as Teach for America and a local teaching residency program. During this time, they relied upon these pipeline programs to fill high numbers of vacancies in all subject areas, and a critical need for science teachers in particular. However, the number of new hires has decreased as a result of the recent economic downturn. Although the city never laid off teachers, it did reduce hiring in all areas and from alternative certification programs in particular during the study period. Moreover, in 2010 William City teachers approved a new contract that uses a variety of measures, including performance evaluations, professional development, and leadership initiatives to indicate progress along career ladders, already complicating traditional visions of career development as rooted in credits earned and seniority.

Data Collection

The research was conducted in two phases. The first phase (for full details please see Rinke, 2009, 2011) included a survey to all first-, second-, and third-year high school science teachers ($N = 73$) in 2005 ($n = 40$, 54.8 percent response rate) and a follow-up survey to initial respondents in 2006 ($n = 23$, 57.4 percent response rate). This survey was intended to characterize the target population as a whole with respect to professional engagement and confidence, workplace context, preparation route, and career plans. From initial survey respondents, eight case study teachers were selected for more in-depth participation.

Participants (see table 1.2) were selected based on stratified purposive sampling using a range of characteristics, including gender, age, race/ethnicity, experience level, subject area, certification route, school culture, and school type. Case study teachers were followed over a period of twelve months and engaged in monthly semistructured interviews (see appendix A for complete interview guide). In addition professional and classroom observations were conducted, intended to capture teachers' life experiences, professional goals, day-to-day rewards and challenges, and interactions in various workplace contexts. These regular meetings were also intended to elucidate any career decision making in progress.

The second phase of the study was conducted six years later, in 2011 and 2012, with the intention of returning to initial participants to understand the development of their career trajectories, based on earlier plans and experiences. Phase 1 survey respondents received a follow-up survey tracking current professional role and career influences (n = 20, 50 percent response rate). In addition, follow-up interviews were conducted with all eight case study teachers to better understand their current professional context, goals, and pathways. Participant and classroom observations were also conducted with case study teachers, when available. The goal of this second study phase was to capture evolving career influences and trajectories both within and outside of classroom teaching.

Data Analysis

Survey data were summarized based on frequency, looking in particular at teachers' priorities with respect to professional growth, student development, and service to society. Teachers' engagement in the profession, with respect to collaboration and participation in professional learning opportunities, was also described. Then, teachers' demographic characteristics and their intentions in the field were compared with their career roles seven years later in an effort to identify relationships between initial and follow-up data. Because of small sample sizes, Fisher's exact tests were conducted to determine the presence of statistically significant associations between teachers' characteristics, initial career plans, and later professional roles (Rea & Parker, 2005).

Table 1.2.   Overview of Case Study Participants at the Initiation of the Study in 2005

Name	Gender	Age	Race	Year	Subject	Certification	School Culture	School Type
Alexandra	Female	20–25	White	2	Bio/Tech	TFA	Moderate	Comprehensive
Alison	Female	25–30	White	3	Chem.	Traditional	Strong	Restructured
Charlotte	Female	25–30	White	1	Physics	Alternative	Weak	Alternative
Denise	Female	20–25	African American	1	Biology	Alternative	Moderate	Comprehensive
Matthew	Male	25–30	White	3	Enviro.	Traditional	Moderate	Reststructured
Mitch	Male	25–30	White	2	Chem.	TFA	Weak	Magnet
Raya	Female	40–45	White	3	Enviro.	Alternative	Weak	Restructured
Tara	Female	30–35	African American	1	Chem.	None	Moderate	Restructured

Notes:
1. Certification route was designated as traditional, defined as an undergraduate or graduate university-based program, or alternative, defined as a program centered outside of a university but which may partner with a university to fulfill certain instructional needs.
2. School culture was determined based on responses to the questions in the school climate portion of the survey. Survey items were selected from the Center for Research on the Context of Teaching published surveys (1991, 2001, 2002). Weak school culture was defined as an average response of less than 3.0, moderate as between 3.0 and 3.5, and strong as greater than 3.5 on the 5-point Likert scale.

Qualitative data were coded based on constructs present in the literature as well as emergent patterns, including categories of personal experiences, workplace context and climate, decision-making processes, efficacy, and career pathways (Merriam, 1998; Yin, 2003). Content analyses were then conducted both within and across cases in order to identify patterns, while maintaining the integrity of the individual's personal and professional experiences (Miles & Huberman, 1994). In analyzing qualitative transcripts, field notes, and artifacts, particular attention was paid to conceptualizing the development of career trajectories as a multifaceted process that involves a complex web of factors, rather than a single variable (Ng & Peter, 2010). In his study of early career attrition, Schaefer (2013) writes that too often research on teacher attrition is focused on answering questions of why teachers leave. He comments:

> Within this focus, teachers' experiences were stripped away with a hope of revealing a solution to the perceived problem of early career teacher attrition. While it is important to better understand *why* early career teachers leave, shifting from thinking about *why* teachers leave, to thinking about *how* they leave, signifies attentiveness towards the temporal unfolding of early career teachers' lives . . . [and offers] glimpses into *how much was at work* in the leaving. (p. 7)

The analysis similarly attempted to authentically capture the process of choosing to stay, shift, or leave by following teachers over time and attending to the evolution of their reasoning about the profession as well as their role in it.

LEARNING FROM TEACHERS IN AN EXPLORATORY CONTEXT

Research tells us that 46 percent of new teachers leave the field during their first five years (Ingersoll, 2003a; Ingersoll & Perda, 2011) and that today's teachers follow career pathways toward continued teaching, education-related roles, or noneducational roles (Donaldson et al., 2008; Quartz et al., 2008). This longitudinal case study indicates that this cohort of urban science teachers very closely follows this broader pattern. Nine of the twenty survey respondents, or 45 percent, remain as classroom teachers today, with an additional six (30 percent) shifting to education-related fields, and the remaining five (25 percent) working outside of the field of education. Of those who are still teaching, six remain in William City or other urban or rural high-need contexts, while three have moved to a suburban or more highly resourced context.

The career trajectories of the eight case study teachers tell much the same story, with three remaining in the classroom, two shifting into education-related positions, and three aspiring to or currently working outside of the field of education (see table 1.3). What is most remarkable about their journeys is the extent to which their initial plans remained consistent over time, the difficult transition many faced as they moved or attempted to move into new workplace contexts, and the determination they exhibited in pursuing efficacy. The chapters that come will capture the professional journeys of William City's science teachers in general, and the eight case study teachers in particular, as they evolved from novice educators to more seasoned professionals of all kinds.

Lessons about Teaching as Exploration

From the experiences of these teachers and former teachers, we learn important lessons about teaching in an exploratory context. First, we learn that when it is no longer inevitable that teachers will enter the classroom at the beginning of their careers and leave thirty years later, and instead teachers' careers can take many varied forms, individual intentions matter. Those teachers who in 2005 planned to enter teaching as a long-term profession may have shifted among school contexts, roles, and responsibilities both within and outside of the classroom, but they almost universally remained within the field of education. Conversely, those teachers who initially planned to pursue teaching as a short-term occupation have since left education for other fields. Teachers' intentions seem to serve as lenses on the field of education that interpret both personal and professional challenges while guiding individuals along differing career trajectories. These intentions also appear to remain surprisingly consistent over time, framing individuals' career decisions in a coherent manner.

Second, we learn that not only is teaching now considered exploratory while entering and exiting the profession, but teaching can also be exploratory during the profession. We find that even those teachers who remain steadfastly committed to classroom teaching or to the field of education continue to explore their professional options. Some seek out better workplace conditions, others greater opportunities for professional growth, and still others closer relationships with students and colleagues. But we find that it is not only new teachers entering the field or disillusioned teachers leaving who explore. Rather, many teachers appear to see exploration as a vital element in career development and choose to explore their way into, through, and at times out of the profession.

Table 1.3. Overview of Case Study Participants at the Conclusion of the Study in 2012

Name	Years Teaching	Initial Plans	Current Role	Additional Training	Level of Satisfaction	Future Plans
Alexandra	8	Short-term	District administrator	Earned master's in public health	Moderate	Enter field of public health
Alison	7	Long-term	District administrator	Earned master's and admin. certificate	High	Possible move to school admin.
Charlotte	4	Short-term	Government defense	Transitional position in info. technology	High	Continue in current role
Denise	7	Long-term	Urban teacher	Earning doctorate in science education	Low	Switch schools or enter higher ed.
Matthew	9	Long-term	Suburban teacher	None	Moderate	Increase inquiry opportunities
Mitch	4	Long-term	Curriculum developer	Possibly ed. leadership	Moderate	Enter school or district leadership
Raya	9	Middle-term	Urban teacher	Professional development	Moderate	Possible move to suburban district
Tara	1	Short-term	Forensic analyst	Earned second bachelor's in forensics	High	Continue in current role

Third, by carefully attending to the ways in which teachers today experience the profession, we find that this new exploratory context can come with high costs not only for students and schools, but also for the teachers themselves. Although alternative certification programs and policy changes have lowered barriers to entry into the field, the road out of teaching can entail extensive retraining, additional graduate degrees, and an extended transitional period. Many of the teachers in the study who planned to explore teaching, coming into the classroom with short-term intentions, also found the work of teaching high-poverty students in urban settings to be physically and emotionally exhausting, necessitating a period of recovery upon leaving the classroom. For these individuals, teaching was in no way an "easy in–easy out" profession. Rather, teaching science in urban schools was a trying and stressful period in the lives of these teachers that did not directly prepare them for their next career steps.

From this research, we find that the exploratory context is neither a positive nor a negative development. There are tangible advantages that come from this new context for teaching, namely the recruitment of a larger, more diverse teaching force with strong expertise in high-need areas such as math and science and an interest in promoting educational equity for all students. Likewise, there are disadvantages to this new context such as higher rates of attrition, lower professional commitment and preparation, and the academic, financial, and personal costs to students, schools, and teachers. From these teachers' experiences, we cannot conclude that the exploratory context should be either promoted or avoided. Rather, we must come to understand the new context and adapt the structures of the profession so all teachers can thrive within it.

One potential approach to effectively managing this exploratory context is to make teachers' intentions, so critical to shaping their later career trajectories, a more explicit part of the recruitment and retention process. This research shows that teachers can effectively articulate their professional plans quite early in their careers and that these plans bear out over the long term. By carefully attending to teachers' intentions in the field and helping them to articulate and examine their plans, we may offer teachers the opportunity to deliberately construct meaningful career pathways. Listening to teachers' ideas about the profession and their role in it may become a central part of structuring the teaching profession in an exploratory context.

John Rury (1989) notes that the transience of teachers has contributed to the historically low status of education in comparison with other professions, writing:

> The identification of teaching with youth, and with a generally transient work force, further distinguished teachers from lawyers, doctors, and other more highly esteemed professionals in popular thinking. De-

spite the commonplace association of teachers with formal education, they have often been held in low regard simply because wisdom and knowledge have been widely regarded in American culture as attributes of experience and age. As long as teaching was largely conducted by young people, it suffered from a persistent image of immaturity and incompetence which perpetuated the notion that teaching was a mere way station for men and women intent on bigger and better things in life. (p. 11)

Ingersoll and Merrill (2012) likewise note that the current exploratory context has the potential to undo years of professionalization efforts for teachers, writing:

A return to an old face could have serious implications for the future stature, standing and status of elementary and secondary teaching in the US . . . Since early in the 20th century, educators have repeatedly sought to upend the notion that teaching is akin to industrial work where teachers are interchangeable and easily replaced, and they have sought to promote the view that teaching is highly complex work, requiring specialized knowledge and skills and deserving of the same status, stature and standing as traditional professions . . . If teaching becomes an even larger, lower-paying line of work, predominantly employing young, inexperienced women, who stay for limited periods, these trends do not suggest optimism for these aspirations. (p. 19)

As we learn to manage this new exploratory context, it is vital that we remain cognizant of the respect afforded to teachers and their contribution to our collective future. As we accept and legitimize the exploratory context, we must assure that exploration becomes a way for professionals to grow and expand their expertise, rather than de-skill the act of teaching. Perhaps by attending more closely to teachers' intentions in the field, we may provide them with the autonomy of professionals and offer an enriching form of exploration.

TWO

Teachers' Plans Matter

We know that today's beginning teachers bring into the classroom a variety of perspectives about teaching and the teaching profession. They also come to the classroom via diverse entry points and preparation routes. What we are still learning is how these initial perspectives matter over time. In this chapter, we meet a group of science teachers who were in their first three years of teaching in the William City Public Schools in 2005. We follow them along their career paths until 2012, where we find that some have remained as teachers in urban schools, some have moved to suburban or private school settings, some have shifted into education-related positions, and still others have left the field entirely. We learn from their experiences that initial career plans are tightly linked to ultimate career pathways, suggesting the tremendous importance of teachers' plans and perspectives on their future trajectories. The experiences of these educators also set the stage for understanding how teachers' intentions mediate their school-based experiences and shape their professional journeys.

TEACHERS' PLANS

Although teachers are generally not asked about their long-term career intentions as part of the standard teacher education or district hiring process, we know that teachers' plans matter in several ways for their later career directions. Previous research has highlighted the role that teachers' motivations, visions, self-understandings, and early classroom experiences play in shaping their ultimate trajectories. While some studies reflect backward upon early ideas that brought teachers into the profession and others project forward on how current ideas are linked to future plans, together they begin to shed light on the important place of

19

early personal and professional inputs upon later professional career pathways.

Australian researchers Helen Watt and Peter Richardson's (2008, 2012) work on the FIT-Choice survey not only synthesizes various motivations for entering teaching and highlights three distinct types of educators, it also links those types to motivations and perceptions about the teaching profession. For instance, Watt and Richardson found that the group of teachers they term highly engaged persisters report being significantly more motivated by the individual and social usefulness of teaching and report significantly higher perceptions of their teaching abilities than the other groups of teachers. These individuals also plan to remain for a career in the classroom.

Conversely, the group of teachers that Watt and Richardson term lower-engaged desisters report the lowest levels of motivation based on individual and social usefulness factors. These individuals largely see teaching as a stepping-stone to other education and non-education-related fields. Their research demonstrates the connection between the personal and social value that teachers place upon their profession and their intentions to stay in the field, with those who hold higher respect for the field also planning to persist for longer.

In the United States, Karen Hammerness (2006) likewise argues that it is not only teachers' motivations which influence their career directions, it is also their visions for classroom practice along with their ability to enact those visions in practice. Defining teachers' visions as vivid and concrete images of practice shaped by both past experiences and current contexts, Hammerness highlights the experiences of teachers whose careers were guided by their pedagogical visions toward a focus on subject matter, student achievement, and social purpose.

Her work also highlights the relationship between the visions teachers bring with them to the classroom and their later career paths. She argues that teachers may switch schools as they seek out more compatible workplace contexts in which to enact their pedagogical visions. She further argues that much movement between schools is pedagogically driven, while movement out of education is frequently more personally motivated, once again emphasizing the role of visions in guiding teachers' careers into, through, and out of classrooms (Hammerness, 2008).

Working with student teachers in Belgium, Isabel Rots and colleagues (Rots, Aelterman, Vlerick, & Vermeulen, 2007; Rots, Kelchtermans, & Aelterman, 2012) expanded the scope of this research to look at the role that prospective teachers' ideas about the profession play in their decisions to pursue a career in teaching. Knowing that approximately half of those trained in education never enter the classroom, Rots and her colleagues investigated the dynamics influencing prospective teachers' decisions to continue pursuing a career in education. They found that two primary factors, prospective teachers' commitment to the profession and their sense of professional competence, were central in influencing their motivation to pursue positions as teachers. Rots and colleagues argue that these factors constitute part of teachers' self-understanding, a more complex and dynamic form of identity, which is central to shaping their career pathways.

Finally, Lindsey Smethem (2007), working in the United Kingdom, highlights the importance of early career experiences in shaping teachers' future plans. Within her typology of career, classroom, and portfolio teachers, Smethem notes that these pathways are shaped by teachers' prior experiences and motivations for teaching. However, she also finds that they can be influenced by early school-based experiences, particularly with respect to increasing workload and role intensification. In particular, negative experiences with workload, students, colleagues, or the broader school culture can diminish plans to stay in the classroom, whereas positive encouragement and the development of a sense of success can instead increase plans for retention. In this way, we find that teachers bring with them ideas and intentions for teaching, but these plans are also molded by school-based experiences.

Taken together, this research underscores our growing understanding of the relationship between inputs and outputs, or the ideas that teachers bring to the classroom and their evolving career pathways. We know that teachers are drawn to teaching for a variety of reasons, and that those influenced by social utility and self-efficacy appear to be connected with a more extended commitment to the classroom. We know that teachers bring with them visions of pedagogical practice and seek out contexts to better enact those visions. We know that preservice teachers' self-understandings influence their decisions to seek out employment in teaching. And we know that early career experiences can shape those initial ideas in both positive and negative ways. Together, these studies paint a picture of teachers' career paths as guided not by singular school-based incidents, but rather by an implicit connection between their ideas about themselves, their pedagogy, and their careers, and the later enactment of those ideas.

In this next section, we will look at the experiences of one cohort of beginning teachers in William City and see what brought them to the classroom, what ideas they held about their roles as educators, and the relationship between these initial ideas and their later career pathways. From these teachers, we come to better understand the connection between teachers' intentions and their trajectories and begin to see how teachers themselves are highly knowledgeable and effective forecasters of their own professional futures.

COMING TO THE CLASSROOM

The remainder of this chapter draws upon the experiences of the cohort of beginning teachers who were in their first, second, or third years of science teaching in the William City Public Schools in the 2005–2006 school year. These teachers, who taught in a variety of traditional neighborhood, restructured, and charter schools, follow national demographic trends, although they reflect somewhat greater diversity (see table 2.1). Overwhelmingly, the average teacher in the United States is White, female, and traditionally prepared (Papay, 2007). This cohort of teachers is more diverse with respect to race/ethnicity, gender, and certification route than the typical teacher.

National Center for Educational Statistics (NCES) data show that in 2007–2008, the most recent year for which data are available, 75.9 percent of teachers in the United States were female and 24.1 percent were male (NCES, 2008). However, in this cohort only 65 percent of teachers were female, and 35 percent male. Likewise, 19 percent of all teachers nationally are prepared via alternative certification pathways. Among these teachers almost three times that number, 55 percent, came from alternative, non-university-based preparation routes, whereas only 45 percent came from traditional programs. These numbers are reflective of the high-need nature of the William City School District. With respect to age, this was a young group, with over 77 percent of the teachers under thirty years of age. Although data on teacher age distributions typically show a U-shaped curve, with many teachers at the lower and the upper ends of the distribution (Papay, 2007), it seems reasonable that among beginning teachers the vast majority would be just starting along their career paths.

This group of teachers was also more diverse ethnically than teachers nationwide, which reflects the largely African American population in this school district and city. Nationally in 2007–2008, 83 percent of teachers were White, 7 percent Black, 1.4 percent Asian/Pacific Islander, and 7.1 percent Hispanic, although in urban areas that number shifts to 71 percent White, 12 percent Black, 2.5 percent Asian/Pacific Islander, and 13.1 percent Hispanic (NCES, 2008). Among this cohort of educators, 56.4 percent were White, 30.8 percent Black, 7.7 percent Asian/Pacific Islander, and 2.6 percent Hispanic. Taken together, this cohort of beginning teachers reflects national trends while also exhibiting greater gender, preparation, and ethnic diversity than the national teacher workforce.

Like all teachers, these beginning educators came to the classroom motivated by a variety of both personal and professional factors and aimed to accomplish a number of goals through their classroom work. The survey contained three separate sections inquiring into teachers' motivations, school choices, and future directions. Together, their responses paint the portrait of a group of beginning teachers deeply committed to developing students, particularly in underserved communities, and mak-

Beginning Teacher Demographics

Gender	Certification Route	Age	Race/Ethnicity
65% Female	45% Traditional	77.5% Under 30	56.4% White
35% Male	55% Alternative	15% 30–39	30.8% African American
		7.5% Over 40	7.7% Asian/Pacific Islander
			2.6% Hispanic

ing a social contribution through their work. They primarily selected their schools based on the school culture and were moderately satisfied with their workplace conditions. While the majority of these teachers saw themselves staying in education, a sizable minority also envisioned leaving the field in the long term.

The first section of the survey asked teachers to rank their professional priorities from "not important" to "very important" using a Likert scale. Teachers indicated what professional goals they saw as the most important aspects of their work. Related to notions of motivation or vision, these priorities reflect what it is that brings teachers to the classroom, what they value in their work, and where they devote the most energy. Of the three priority categories, *professional growth, student development,* and *service,* teachers appeared to value their own professional growth less than their students' development and their potential contribution to society. Where teachers did value their own professional growth, it was primarily in classroom-based contexts, in their work as classroom instructors and managers, as well as collaborators (see figure 2.1), where 95 percent, 95 percent, and 77.5 percent respectively of teachers indicated these areas were very important to their work. Teachers in general tend to underestimate the personal rewards of their work in favor of benefits to students, at least publically, and these results reinforce that pattern.

Rather than focusing on their own professional growth, these beginning teachers instead indicated that several aspects of student development were top priorities (see figure 2.2). Developing student self-discipline ranked the highest, with 100 percent of participating teachers indicating it was a very important aspect of their work. Increasing student subject-matter knowledge was also highly valued, at 92.5 percent, as was developing student self-confidence at 90 percent, strengthening basic reading, writing, and mathematics skills at 82.5 percent, and test preparation at 75 percent. Positive citizenship and enthusiasm for learning were seen as less critical student development priorities.

Participating teachers also viewed service to society as a central priority in their work (see figure 2.3), with 97.5 percent of teachers indicating that support for the underserved was very important. They also highly ranked the ideas of being a role model and making a difference in society, with 92.5 percent of teachers indicating both were very important aspects

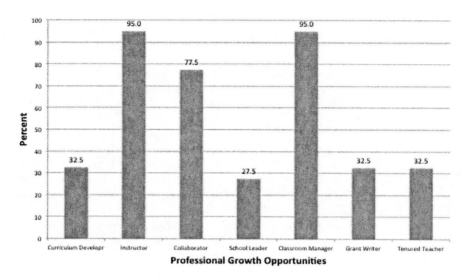

Figure 2.1.   Percentage of Teachers Ranking Professional Growth Priorities as "Very Important"

of their work. Giving back to society, at 70 percent, and influencing school reform, at 67.5 percent, were also critical professional priorities. While the intrinsic value of teaching has been shown time and time again to be an important motivating factor for teachers (e.g., Lortie, 1975; Watt et al., 2012; Yee, 1990), it seems reasonable that these teachers who specifically selected teaching positions in a high-need district with large numbers of low-income students value their contribution not only to their students but also to larger society.

NAVIGATING THE SCHOOL CONTEXT

As part of the survey, beginning science teachers were also asked to rank the various factors that influenced their choice of a specific teaching position within the larger field (for details, see figure 2.4). While slightly over one-quarter of the teachers reported being placed at their school by the district or their alternative certification program, others reported various positive features of the school site. For instance, 33.1 percent of participating teachers indicated that extrinsic benefits such as salary and compatibility with family life were very important in their position selection and 34.2 percent reported being drawn to certain curriculum approaches, such as a particular academic or extracurricular program. The largest number, 38.5 percent of teachers, selected their schools because of a positive sense of the school culture, with respect to students, teachers, and

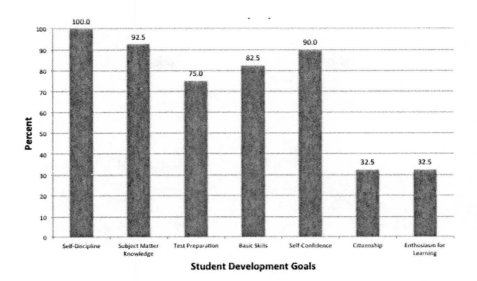

Figure 2.2.   Percentage of Teachers Ranking Student Development Priorities as "Very Important"

administration, reinforcing what we already know about the centrality of school culture to teachers' work lives (e.g., Johnson, Kraft, & Papay, 2012; Rosenholtz & Simpson, 1990).

Once at their school, these teachers were active and engaged professionals. They reported participating in seventeen separate professional activities on either a weekly or monthly basis, everything from curriculum collaboration to professional development and from university coursework to extracurricular activities with their students. Overall, 82 percent of these teachers felt that they participated in either the same number or more professional activities than their peers within the same school building.

Despite what is often reported as the challenging conditions of urban teaching, these teachers were also not unsatisfied with their school cultures (see figure 2.5). When asked to agree or disagree with statements about their school, a majority of participating teachers, 54.5 percent, strongly agreed with the idea that their schools represented professional learning communities. They also felt there were opportunities for professional collaboration, with 43.8 percent strongly agreeing that they worked within a collaborative environment. Only 18.8 percent of teachers felt that they worked within a strongly bureaucratic school culture. Overall, 37.5 percent of these teachers reported being highly satisfied with their school context, while only 22.5 percent were highly dissatisfied with their day-to-day work conditions. Taken together, these results paint a

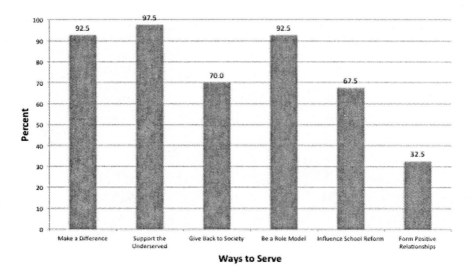

Figure 2.3.   Percentage of Teachers Ranking Service Priorities as "Very Important"

picture of schools not at the extremes, but somewhere in the middle, with certain strengths such as collaboration but also important areas for growth. They also show this cohort of teachers to be moderately satisfied with their working conditions.

PLANNING FOR THE FUTURE

When beginning science teachers were surveyed during the 2005–2006 school year, they already had ideas about where their careers were headed, with some envisioning long-term careers in the classroom, some hoping to shift into educational leadership or education-related roles, and still others planning to leave education altogether for unrelated career paths (captured in figure 2.6).

Although there was some fluidity among the groups, reflecting a degree of uncertainty about future directions, overall 15.6 percent of participants planned to remain as classroom teachers over the long term and were about evenly split between continuing in a high-need urban context and moving to a more well-resourced environment. A larger group, 29.4 percent, saw themselves as shifting into some type of education-related role, including mentor teacher, school or district leader, or policy advocate. The largest group of all, 42.5 percent of teachers, planned to eventually move out of the field of education. A final group is noteworthy for its small size; only 2.5 percent of these teachers indicated that they would

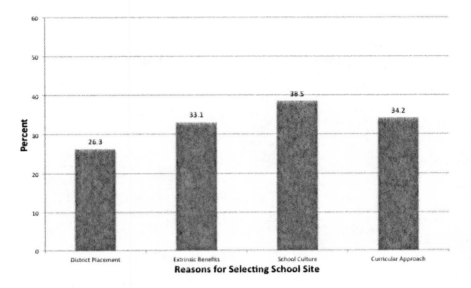

Figure 2.4.   Percentage of Teachers Ranking School Features as "Very Important"

like someday to become stay-at-home parents, challenging the traditional conception of female teachers as interweaving years of classroom work with years of home-based child rearing (Biklen, 1995).

These data raise the question of whether this largely alternatively certified group of new teachers exclusively see education as a transient occupation. Although conclusions are unclear, some previous research has suggested that teachers who enter the classroom via alternative pathways are less committed to education and stay for shorter periods of time (Shen, 1998), although it has been questioned whether these higher attrition rates are due to lack of commitment or inadequate preparation (Johnson, Berg, & Donaldson, 2005). This survey suggests that while traditionally prepared teachers are highly committed to teaching and education-related work, the majority of alternatively prepared teachers also are looking for a convenient way to contribute to the field of education.

Among this cohort of teachers, 88.8 percent of the traditionally certified teachers planned to continue in classroom teaching or an education-related position over time. However, 64.2 percent of the alternatively certified teachers also hoped to remain in education-related roles long-term, with only 35.8 percent of alternate-route educators planning to ultimately leave the field. These results suggest that while some of this exploratory dynamic is certainly due to the proliferation of alternative certification pathways, it cannot entirely be attributed to these abbreviated

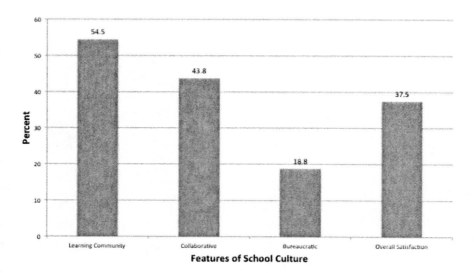

Figure 2.5.   Percentage of Teachers "Strongly Agreeing" with Features of School Climate

preparation routes since the majority of these alternatively certified teachers hoped to become career educators.

CARRYING OUT THEIR PLANS

When this same cohort of teachers was surveyed seven years later, in 2012, respondents had pursued all three major career trajectories—classroom teaching, education-related roles, and noneducational positions (illustrated in figure 2.7). More specifically, the largest group, 47.8 percent of teachers, currently held teaching positions, with 60 percent remaining within William City or another high-need district and 40 percent shifting to a more well-resourced context. A smaller group, 21.8 percent, had moved into education-related roles, with over two-thirds working at the William City district office in leadership positions. Others had shifted into teacher preparation and educational policy. Finally, 30.4 percent of participants reported moving out of education entirely, working primarily in health care and government.

These teachers' experiences largely paralleled national trends. Ingersoll (2003a) notes that 46 percent of beginning teachers in the United States leave the classroom within their first five years. This cohort of educators, working in a high-need district, had a somewhat higher attrition rate with 52.2 percent of teachers moving out of the classroom within a seven-year window. They did tend to stay longer than expected, however, with almost half of the leavers remaining in teaching for six to nine

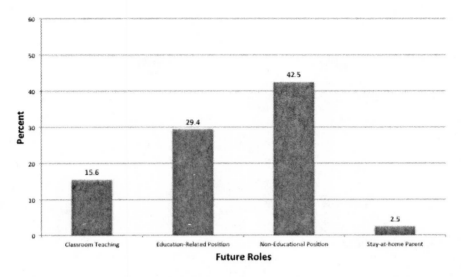

Figure 2.6.   Percentage of Teachers Reporting Future Roles as "Very Likely" in 2005

years before moving on. Their experiences also reflect the larger theme of dissatisfaction with teaching, particularly among science teachers (Ingersoll, 2003b).

Almost half of the teachers who left, 47.4 percent, cited dissatisfaction with their workplace context, school community, or leadership as the primary factor motivating their decisions to leave. Desire to pursue career alternatives was also important, at 31.6 percent, possibly owing to the low status and prestige of a teaching career. Only 15.8 percent of teachers cited salary and 10.5 percent reported personal influences as primary factors in their departure. These findings tend to reflect the current culture of deemphasizing financial and personal influences in teachers' career decisions (e.g., Johnson, 2004; Lankford, Loeb, & Wyckoff, 2002).

The most striking finding comes from a closer analysis of the relationship between individual teachers' plans and their later professional roles. Based on their original survey results in 2005, teachers were grouped into two dichotomous categories: internally focused on the field of education and externally focused on other fields. Teachers who responded that they were very likely to pursue either teaching or education-related positions like school or district leadership were categorized as internally focused at the beginning of their careers. Those who responded that they were very likely to pursue a non-education-related field were categorized as externally focused.

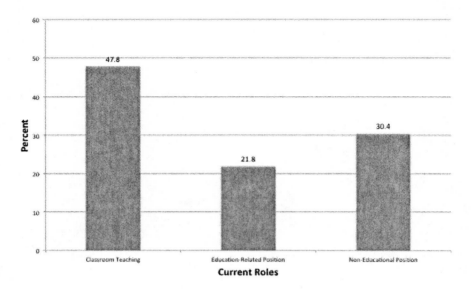

Figure 2.7.   Percentage of Teachers Holding Professional Roles in 2012

No value judgment was intended in these categories; they were simply meant to be descriptive of where the teachers' original intentions lay with respect to their future careers. Ivor Goodson (1991) discusses the notion of a center of gravity which teachers use to organize and make sense of their professional lives. Internally and externally focused intentions are meant to reflect this idea of a professional center of gravity for these teachers.

An analysis of the relationship between teachers' initial plans and their later roles showed that 100 percent of internally focused teachers remained in education seven years later. While some were no longer teaching, none had left the field of education as a whole. Likewise, 75 percent of externally focused teachers had left the field of education as originally planned. Only 25 percent of the externally focused group remained in education, modifying their initial plans. A Fisher's exact test, selected because of the small sample size, with Bonferroni correction to account for multiple comparisons, found this association to be statistically significant at the 0.01 level.

These results suggest that teachers actually stuck quite closely to their originally intended pathways. Although there was some movement between classroom teaching and education-related positions based on working conditions and professional opportunities, those who intended to stay in education largely did so, whereas those who intended to someday leave also followed through on their original plans.

An e-mail communication with one of the few externally focused teachers who reported teaching seven years later showed that her path was highly circuitous and in fact her return to the classroom stemmed more from her temporary desire for a family-friendly career while her child was young than any change of professional orientation. When asked about her experiences, this teacher described a career route that included three years of classroom teaching followed by work at a private learning center, application and acceptance to medical school, and finally a return to education. Despite the fact that she has currently returned to classroom teaching, she still remains externally focused on other work-life options, writing, "I'm happy here now, but I may leave again in the future, when I get bored or fed up or to be a stay-at-home mom. I might have made a different decision, but the hours that a teacher keeps are ideal for raising small children." This teacher's experience suggests that even among those who modify existing plans, initial orientations hold strong over time.

Also interesting is the finding that so many of the traditional factors understood to be related to teachers' career pathways were not significantly associated with later career directions. For instance, several studies have documented that younger teachers, especially those under the age of thirty, leave the profession at higher rates, as do White teachers and, as previously discussed, alternatively certified educators (Bobbitt, Faupel, & Burns, 1991; Boe, Bobbitt, Cook, Whitener, & Weber, 1997; Dworkin, 1980; Shen, 1998). The results of this survey showed that none of these factors—age, race/ethnicity, and certification route—were significantly associated with teachers' current roles within or outside of education based on Fisher's exact tests. Likewise, teachers' engagement in the profession, as measured by level of participation in professional activities, also did not show a statistically significant association with later career direction. Although the strength of these associations certainly was influenced by small sample size, it is nonetheless interesting given the strong association between original orientation and later professional role.

Also interesting is participants' plans for their next steps, from 2012 forward. Those teachers who left the field of education largely plan to continue along their career paths, responding, "I hope to be advancing in my career" or "continue in current position," echoing related research showing that teachers who have left the field are largely satisfied with their decisions (Buchanan, 2009).

However, those who remained in teaching almost exclusively aimed to take on additional leadership or mentorship roles down the road, responding that they hoped to "move to the level of adult certification as soon as possible," "teach other science teachers," "be in a position of educational leadership," "teach at a community college," and "become involved in science curriculum development." While some of these positions could certainly be pursued simultaneously with classroom teaching, others would require a shift into an education-related position. This suggests that those who have chosen a career in the field of education do not want to be left out of opportunities for professional growth and the chance to take on new roles, responsibilities, and challenges over time.

Finally, the 2012 follow-up survey inquired about the influence of the larger economy on teachers' career decisions. Starting in 2008, the United States faced difficult economic conditions that resulted in teacher layoffs, although not locally in William City, as well as slow hiring and few opportunities in other fields. Despite these challenging conditions, very few of the participants who shifted to education-related positions or out of education altogether reported that the economy had any influence on their decision making, with 81.8 percent of these participants reporting that it had no influence or very little influence and the other 18.2 percent reporting some influence upon their career pathways. While the majority of those still teaching agreed, there was a more sizable minority, 37.5 percent, who suggested that the economy had some influence or a very large influence over their career directions. Their responses highlight the notion that while the economy may have been one of many factors acting upon teachers' career trajectories during this time, it acted to inflate the retention rate rather than reduce it as teachers shied away from leaving the security of their school positions.

TEACHERS' PLANS MATTER

Typically when we speak with teachers about their careers, we project forward or reflect backward in their careers from a single point in time. These survey results are unique in that they longitudinally track individuals as they develop their careers over a seven-year period. It is clear that this group of teachers, who began teaching science in a high-need district in 2005, came into the classroom fully immersed in the exploratory context. Most of them were young, under thirty years of age; they came from more diverse racial/ethnic backgrounds than teachers nationwide; and the majority arrived via alternative certification pathways. They also held lofty ideals for the profession, prioritizing student development and service while seeking positive school climates for their work. And they knew right from the start where they were headed. Those who intended to stay within the field of education might have shifted between teaching and leadership roles, but they stayed within education, whereas those who saw teaching as more of a temporary pursuit taught for some time and then moved on.

The survey results demonstrate that these teachers were able to predict their career paths within their first three years in the field, plans that largely materialized over time. In this way, we have our first example of the ways in which inputs matter. Teachers' plans for their own professional direction matter because they capture where teachers see themselves several years down the road and what they hope to accomplish as professionals. They serve as implicit guides as teachers develop their career trajectories over time. And these results suggest that their own plans are far more reliable predictors of retention, at least in the field of education overall if not in the classroom per se, than traditional notions of demographics or even working conditions. They also reframe the debate about teachers' careers so that teachers are seen as active agents constructing their own professional futures, rather than more passive vehicles subject to forces beyond their own control.

As we will see in the coming case studies, teachers' plans also matter because they shape teachers' responses to and management of the school context. The case studies show that teachers come to the profession with ideas, shaped by years of experience with their families and schools, about what it means to be a teacher in today's society. Building upon notions of teacher motivations, visions, and self-understandings (e.g., Hammerness, 2006; Rots et al., 2007; Watt & Richardson, 2008), these ideas guide teachers as they negotiate school-based interactions and develop their career trajectories.

Certainly workplace conditions positively or negatively influence their attitudes and plans within the teaching profession, but their conceptions of the profession hold steady. Those who view teaching as a prestigious and valuable profession retain that perspective despite challenges, whereas those who feel that teaching is a worthwhile but undervalued temporary occupation likewise hold on to these ideas over time. The case studies show that some teachers managed their work lives and stayed in the classroom by focusing on what was meaningful, others by shifting into education-related roles when important relationships soured, and still others by viewing challenges as a sign that it was time to change course.

THREE

Those Who Stayed

I'm prepared for the heat. The only thing they didn't change is the heat.
— Denise, starting her second year in the classroom

Of the eight case studies, all beginning teachers in urban science class-rooms in 2005, three remained in teaching positions seven years later, although none at their original school site. Denise continued to teach biology in William City but transferred to a different school, seeking better working conditions in general and newer facilities in particular. Frustrated with his ability to make an impact in urban schools, Matt accepted a position in a neighboring suburban district, where he continues to connect with students through athletics. Finally, Raya also continues teaching in William City, now at her third school. After briefly considering other career directions, she reinvested in teaching and remains a highly engaged professional.

In the cases that follow, we will see how each educator remaining in the classroom constructed individual ways of making meaning from their work. In particular, each of these teachers found some aspect of their work lives, either within or outside of the classroom, where they thrived and made an important contribution. By finding what Matt likes to call their "niches," these teachers valued and respected their own roles as educators. And finally, each of these teachers continued to grow as a professional over time, exploring different roles and responsibilities in career pathways as dynamic as those who left.

DENISE

Denise spent most of her childhood in New York City, the oldest child in a family that included her mother and three younger brothers. Her mother stressed the importance of getting an education, making sure that her children attended school each and every day. Denise explained, "We grew up and school was school. It was like, you go to school. I never woke up and was like, I'm not going to go to school today, because you didn't even ask. You just went to school."

Part of a large family, Denise felt that she needed something to make her stand out, and what distinguished her was that she was smart. A top student throughout school, Denise so surprised one school administration with her outstanding transcript that they thought the school records had been mixed up. Denise explained, "They kept saying they lost [my records] because they didn't believe that they were my grades, because they were all As, and two or three Bs. I think my GPA was 3.8. So they kept saying they lost [my records]." In addition to excelling in her classes, Denise also enjoyed being part of the school cheerleading squad throughout her high school years.

When Denise's mother passed away just before her senior year, Denise and her brothers moved in with their grandmother. Although Denise did not think she had enough money to attend college, her grandmother insisted: "My grandmother was like, you're going to college so you need to pick one." Denise applied to a number of historically black colleges and universities (HBCUs) and ultimately accepted a spot at an HBCU in William City.

However, Denise did not have all of the money she needed to start her first semester, so her family and friends sponsored a raffle to raise the remaining amount and successfully sent her off to college. Denise explained, "I didn't have enough money to pay for college; we still owed $1,600 for my first semester. So we had a raffle, people bought tickets, and they paid for me to come to school. People was [sic] buying like hundreds of raffle tickets." Once she got to school, Denise explained that she worked extra hard because "I don't want to disappoint all these people when they sent me here." Four years later, Denise became the first person in her family to graduate with a four-year college degree.

Exploring Career Paths

As a child, Denise always wanted to be a teacher and spent hours playing school with her younger brothers. However, Denise was discouraged by her family from entering education because of the low pay in the field. She explained, "We were just always playing school. You know algebra, we used to do it with letters, like a + b = c and we used to make up stuff like that when were young. I just felt like that's what I wanted to do. But then people would say, oh, they don't make no money, so I chose something else." Determined to enter a field she considered easy, where she would be able to make a lot of money, Denise elected to major in biology and explored various career options, from medicine to pharmacy to research. She also took advantage of many opportunities available to her during college, conducting research on eye diseases in labs both within and outside of her institution and attending a national conference for minorities in science.

However, Denise rejected all of her previous career options one by one. She explained, "First I thought, oh doctors make money, I'll do that. But then I don't like blood, so that wouldn't work. Then I tried research and I lost interest, so that ain't gonna work either." At the conclusion of college, unsure of her next steps, Denise returned to the idea of teaching and applied to a local alternative certification program in William City. She was accepted, attended a summer training institute in the sweltering heat, and started in her own classroom a few months after college graduation. She commented, "I ended up back where I wanted to be."

Expanding Her Role In and Out of the Classroom

Denise took a position at a large, comprehensive high school on the eastern edge of the city because she was impressed with the dedication and enthusiasm of the school's dynamic science department chair. Although Denise was one of twenty new teachers her first year, there was also a large cohort of seasoned educators at the school who mentored her by providing materials, curriculum ideas, and test preparation strategies. The department chair gathered all the science teachers together every Friday afternoon to share resources and discuss ways to prepare their students for upcoming standardized tests. Denise was also pleased that although she did not teach in a laboratory classroom, her department chair was more than willing to purchase necessary materials when she requested them.

During that first year, Denise felt like she was part of a teaching team, with a common schedule and curriculum designed to prepare all of their students for the high-stakes biology exam. She noted that the other teachers were, " . . . very helpful. I always go to them and ask for suggestions, and I ask them just to see, am I saying this right, or am I doing this right?" In addition to feeling supported by the veteran teachers within her school building, Denise also shared her day-to-day challenges with other new teachers in her building and from her alternative certification program, where they commiserated over lack of resources and student behavioral challenges at regular happy hours and other gatherings.

During her early years in the classroom, Denise forged a strong bond with her students. Impeccably behaved while in her classroom, Denise seemed to exhibit a natural authority that resonated with her students. When one student or another pushed back, Denise was almost always able to bring them on board by appealing to their interests. She described how she built a positive relationship with one challenging student:

> I had a student, man, she didn't do anything for me in the beginning. Nothing. She'd just come in and read her books and stuff. And I asked her to try. I'm like, "Why don't you do anything?" And then everybody said she had a death in her family. I'm like, OK, so do I, but that's life. So I gave her an assignment to read this book called *Hot Zone.* If you read this, then you'll get extra credit. Because I knew she liked to read, and it was dealing with science. So I think we've built a relationship on that. She bought me all types of gifts for Christmas, she kept saying, "Put this on your tree."

Although some of Denise's students persisted with extended absences from school, those who showed up worked diligently in her classroom.

Denise also connected with many students outside of the classroom, which she felt emerged from their common background and shared interests. She noted, "We got things to talk about and I think they feel like I'm reachable. I always talk to them about college and try and be the example. I grew up in the city, and we were poor, so, well, you can do it because I did it." Denise explained that she saw her most important responsibility as a teacher to be simply "listening to those kids. Just listening to everything that they say. They need so much attention, oh my gosh."

And Denise provided many opportunities to listen, as she chatted with students before school, during lunch, and after school about the ups and downs of their lives. She noted, "I have a few that cling to me," elaborating, "They just come all day. They just want to talk. They just want to come in and tell me about their boyfriend, or tell me what they did this weekend, or tell me about this teacher that did something. They just want to talk." At the end of her first year, Denise's photograph was published in the student newspaper, where she was listed as one of the seniors' favorite teachers.

Denise quickly became active in the life of her school, supporting students in a number of fundraisers, volunteering her time as the assistant coach for the cheerleading squad, and attending the school prom to see her students dressed their best. She developed interactive activities such as ecology scavenger hunts, frog dissections, and health challenges. And her students scored among the highest in her school on the annual biology exam. Denise took advantage of numerous professional development opportunities available to her, catching her own fish for a classroom aquarium and enrolling in an extended summer workshop to enhance her biology content knowledge.

While at times Denise questioned whether teaching was the right career choice, for the most part she was headed down the path toward becoming a successful education professional. Denise envisioned herself staying in the classroom for several more years and then transitioning first to department chair and later to school principal. She began talking about continuing on past her teaching master's for a more advanced degree in educational leadership and someday even opening her own school. And she began looking to buy a home in William City through a federally subsidized program for teachers, with her students encouraging her to move in down the street.

Facing Initial Challenges

Despite her successes within and outside of the classroom and her strong commitment to the field of education, Denise's first few years of teaching were not without their challenges. First, Denise worked in un-questionably dilapidated school facilities, with rundown desks and chairs, little sunlight, and contaminated drinking water. She taught sci-ence in a classroom without running water and only one electrical outlet. It was not until her second year that Denise had access to a computer, and only then because a colleague quietly passed it along to her after leaving the school. And her school had no air-conditioning and poor heating, so that she and her students suffered through oppressive heat in the fall and spring and freezing cold in the winter. Although she was more prepared after her first year, filling her classroom with electric fans, teaching was often a physically uncomfortable experience.

Second, Denise was at times frustrated with decisions made by the school and district administration. For one, after spending a full summer mastering the biology curriculum, Denise returned to school in the fall to discover that the district had decided to replace the prior curriculum with a new program. She was instructed to stop using her old materials and teach exclusively with the new system, despite the fact that the textbooks and laboratory supplies had yet to arrive, and once they did arrive were in short supply. Moreover, in her second year Denise coped with the arrival of a new school administrator who, she explained, was "trying to discipline the teachers and students."

Denise butted heads with this woman over morning sign in, use of the copier, and her abundance of forms. The administrator ultimately claimed that Denise "defied her authority" and was "uncooperative," such that Denise decided to avoid interacting with her at all costs. Denise explained, "I just ignore her. I don't have anything to say to her. I just don't want to be bothered because I just feel like that was really rude and unprofessional, and her is trying to make me seem like I did all of these horrible things." Although they ultimately came to a satisfactory truce, this administrator colored Denise's sense of her school as a supportive environment for teachers.

Perhaps worst of all, for Denise, was the pervasive sense that if stu-dents made it to their senior year, they inherently deserved to pass her class and graduate from high school. She explained, "It's a lot of pressure to pass these seniors, and they don't deserve to pass. I just don't like feeling like I have to pass everybody when they don't deserve it. If they try, of course, but just to give it to them, I think that defeats the purpose of me being here." Denise was asked to develop "work packets" for failing students to complete on their own in order to earn the necessary credit for her course, although she commented, "I just don't think that a work packet is going to suffice for a year of work." The common practice ran deeply counter to her principles, and she noted, "I don't think it should be my responsibility for these kids to pass. I think it should be their parents who should be the one on their back." Although she stood up against the practice of work packets to students, parents, and administrators, she ultimately felt that she had no choice but to provide them because when she resisted, her superiors simply went over her head. Denise still held a deep respect for her department chair, but began to realize, "it's just the system, you know. It's above her."

Taking on Leadership Roles

Despite these and other ongoing challenges, Denise persisted as a biology teacher at the same school for a total of six years, growing from a novice teacher into a more seasoned professional. She continued to pursue professional development opportunities, such as a trip to Costa Rica to learn about rainforest ecology, and took on leadership roles like mentoring newer teachers in her alternative certification program. Her students consistently earned among the highest scores in the district on their standardized tests, with a high of 83 percent passing the biology exam. She also organized an annual school-wide science fair and sponsored a colloquium to honor the family of a local African American scientific leader. During this time, Denise also married a fellow William City teacher and bought a home in the area.

It is no surprise, with these successes, that Denise was selected by the William City school district to serve as a teacher leader. In this role, Denise taught half the day and spent the other half working with struggling teachers across the district. She supported them on classroom management, unit planning, and developing more authentic experiences in science. Denise found this work as a teacher leader to be particularly rewarding, commenting, "I like working with teachers because I could share my experience with things that don't work. I feel like I could relate to them." Moreover, they appreciated her guidance. She explained, "I got a good response from the teachers I worked with, too. One of the teachers, he ended up getting the highest [test] scores in the school, and it was his first year. So he wrote me a good letter saying how I helped him do that. That was nice." Encouraged by a colleague and buoyed by her positive experiences as a teacher mentor, Denise also began a doctoral program in science education at her alma mater, taking night classes over a period of several years as she pursued this advanced degree.

Seeking a Better Workplace Context

Although Denise talked for many years about leaving her school in search of a more supportive environment, that time finally came after six years in the classroom. With her principal fired and her department chair retiring, Denise decided to look across the district for a more positive school culture. Denise remained committed to teaching in William City, noting, "I want to stay in the city because I feel like that's where the need is." However, she sought out a more cohesive school context, explaining, "I really like helping the kids and I really like working with the kids, so I would want to be in an environment where everybody feels the same thing. That's my overall goal."

Moreover, with her teacher leader position eliminated by the district, Denise wanted "more support for the classroom, and discipline, and just better leadership." She attended the transfer fair and was attracted to a citywide vocational school because of its high test scores. It was only later that she learned the secret to these surprisingly high scores: The school only permitted passing students to sit for the exam. Denise explained, "When I looked here, they had good [test] scores, so I thought it would be a good place to come and see, oh, they have really good [test] scores so they must have some positive things going on. But they only let people passing the class take the test. So now I'm like, oh okay, now that makes sense." Thinking at the time that high test scores indicated a more positive school culture, Denise transferred within the district to this new high school.

Certain aspects of Denise's new position were vastly improved: The school facilities in her new building were far superior, with shining new desks and a mini-laboratory space in her classroom. She had air-conditioning and could regulate her own heat, so "it's more comfortable." Also, the teaching schedule was organized into sixty-minute rather than ninety-minute blocks, so she had more time available for planning each day. Despite these improvements, Denise was disappointed with the climate at her new school, commenting, "It's nice here. The facilities are nice. But I just don't like it."

Overall, Denise feels that her work with students was not supported at this new school. For one, she sensed that students have the run of the building, explaining, "I just feel like they don't really have any control of the students. Students are always in the hallway doing whatever they want. And they say they're trying to stop these practices, but they're not. Like, oh, send them here, but when you send them, nobody does anything." Also, Denise felt that she could not count on the school leadership. In one such incident, Denise explained:

> I sent an e-mail last week asking for a student's phone number for my new class, and I got an e-mail today. I sent it last Tuesday. I just got the e-mail today saying, oh well, did you look at the student management

system? And I'm like, yeah I looked at the student management system. The number is wrong. That's why I sent you an e-mail last week. And you still didn't even send me a phone number.

Overall, Denise did not feel that the school culture was set up to support her work with students.

Moreover, despite her years of classroom experience and previous role as a district-wide teacher leader, Denise felt that her educational expertise was undervalued. Rather than adopt new ideas from Denise, her department chair insisted on modeling instruction after a previously successful teacher. Denise explained:

> I don't feel like they use me at all. I feel like my department head, she has somebody who had really high [test] scores. I guess he had the highest in the city, something like that last year, and she just expects us to do everything he did. And I don't even know him. He doesn't even work here anymore. He left last year to go to medical school. She always asks, "Oh, what do you think about this?" and then you tell her and she says, "Well, last year, we did this. So we're going to do it like we did last year." It's always about last year.

Moreover, Denise was disappointed that so little money had been spent on science supplies that could be used by students. She commented:

> They said as far as funding, oh, whatever you need, we can order. But I've asked for things and I can't get anything. I know they have money in the budget to finance things. You have to have some money in the budget. What are you doing with the money? If you're not using it, why can't we get some things that we need? We always end up spending our own money. But I don't want to have to spend my own money.

Denise was distressed when she witnessed her department chair spending school funds on retirement parties for colleagues rather than on materials that directly reached students.

Finally, Denise felt that as she got older, it became more and more difficult to connect with her students. While she was once the young teacher they could relate to easily, Denise now found it more challenging to build those same out-of-classroom relationships. She commented, "I feel like I'm getting more disconnected from the kids. I think because I'm getting older, now I can't connect. I don't feel like I'm relating as much to them, but the content, I think, is solid." Now, Denise appeared to make strong connections not with students but instead with newer teachers.

Determining Next Steps

Although only partway through her first year at the new high school, Denise had already resolved to keep moving until she found the supportive school climate she was looking for, commenting, "I just decided I'm just going to keep moving until I find something that I like." She ideally would like a school with a greater focus on academic achievement and stronger school leadership, explaining, "I just want to work with students that want to be successful, and I'm not struggling every day. And if I am, then somebody is going to be there to support me." Plus, she would like to be in a more positive school climate, noting, "There is not people in the hallways smoking or just dropping their food. It's just you actually could move out of the hallway. They move and we don't have to argue about it."

One of her previous mentees was actively recruiting her to come and join him in a biomedical program at one of the more academic citywide schools, and Denise also planned to attend this year's transfer fair to see what other options existed within the district. However, with the imminent completion of her doctoral program Denise was also considering a shift out of the schools and into teacher education. She recognized that it might be challenging to find a job in higher education unless she was willing to relocate. Moreover, although she enjoyed working with new teachers, she was concerned about the other job responsibilities, commenting, "I want to do teacher training type of stuff, but I have to be willing to do the research and I don't know if I want to do that." With these options on her horizon, Denise intended to figure out her next steps as an education professional.

MATT

Born in Hawaii, Matt spent several years living in California and Virginia before moving with his family to Kenya for the majority of his childhood. While his father worked as an auditor for a governmental development agency and his mother raised the children, Matt and his brother attended a highly regarded international school with students from fifty-five countries around the world. A self-described "class clown," Matt nonetheless flourished in this environment, particularly because of its proximity to nature. Matt went with his family on safari almost every weekend and was even informally adopted by a pair of teachers at his school, who also took him to see wildlife. He explained, "There were a couple of teachers who kind of took me under their wing. They wanted to go on field trips on the weekend, and they invited me out. It was just really cool." Even before he moved to Africa, Matt was attracted to nature, explaining, "I used to play in the creek literally every single day, catching snakes, salmon, all that stuff." The six years spent in Kenya solidified his initial affinity into a lifelong passion for wildlife biology.

Matt returned to the United States after his ninth-grade year and attended a large public high school, where he struggled to readjust to the culture and reduced academic expectations. Matt explained:

Total culture shock in 10th grade when I came back. I started off as a good student, but I didn't try as much. I definitely adapted to my environment. I didn't try to act like a slacker; I still did the work. But I didn't push myself. I definitely didn't feel challenged. I always look back and say, if I had stayed in Kenya I think things would have been a little bit different.

While many of his international school peers went off to top universities around the world, eventually earning doctorate, medical, and law degrees, Matt felt that his career choice was less prestigious in comparison, noting, "I'm happy being a teacher, but maybe I would have wanted to be a doctor, or maybe I would have wanted to be a lawyer. I don't know. I would have pushed myself a little bit more, instead of settling to be a teacher."

Finding a Path into Teaching

Nonetheless, Matt followed his passion for being outside and exploring nature into his current career, noting, "That was my goal. What can I do outside working with animals? I was pretty optimistic and wide-eyed and just, I'm gonna save the world." He initially pursued a wildlife biology degree in Colorado, but transferred after the first year to a local state school for the in-state tuition. After college Matt worked with a wildlife-focused nonprofit but was frustrated with the office lifestyle, noting, "I was in a cubicle, behind a computer all day, writing out wildlife Internet plans for corporations that were trying to get some wildlife stuff on their websites. Got bored with that." Next Matt tried field research, working with prairie dogs and falcons in Utah, but found that lifestyle also did not suit him, noting:

I didn't enjoy that either. It was monotonous work, just going around identifying the plants in one area, and go to another area and do the same thing. Habitat surveys and counting prairie dogs and things like that. It's just boring. It gets old doing the same thing over and over again. I never knew that, I didn't know any biologists growing up. It just seemed cool working with animals.

In addition, Matt's field research position was only seasonal and his father was pressuring him to find something more stable with which to build a future career.

Inspired by positive experiences working with children as a camp counselor and the possibility of making a difference in young lives, Matt decided to go into teaching, explaining:

So when I was doing this wildlife stuff I'm thinking, man, I'm not that into wildlife. I love to do it. I love hiking. I love all that stuff. But I can do that stuff on my own, on the weekends. But I really like working

with the kids. Kids, I always had a connection with them somehow. I
felt like I was making a difference in their lives.

He liked the idea of extending his impact beyond what was possible in a
camp environment, noting, "Camp counseling, the kids would come for a
week, maybe two weeks, and then they're gone. So I wanted to have
them for a longer period of time. A semester or a year." Matt enrolled in a
yearlong master's certification program in William City and completed
his student teaching in two separate high schools within the district. He
specifically chose to work in an urban environment because "I felt like I
had to make more of a difference in their lives. They needed people,
especially males and father figures, older brothers, something. A male
role model."

After completing his degree, Matt accepted a position teaching environmental science at a newly restructured high school in the city and
noted, "I don't want to teach anything else. I get to teach what I'm passionate about. I always wanted to stay in wildlife biology; now at least I
get to teach it." In addition, his father was finally pleased with his career
choice. Matthew explained, "They've never been happy with anything
I've done, really. And teaching environmental science is a good fit because they're happy and I'm happy. So I'm not making a whole bunch of
money, but the benefits are good. I wasn't doing some seasonal job. I
wasn't unstable. So it was just a good fit." Matt's father was particularly
impressed with the benefits and encouraged him to start putting money
away for the long term. Matt explained that now his father "gets to say,
my son's a teacher. He respects teachers. Since I became a teacher, he was
like, Matt, I'm really proud of you. I like what you're doing. That's really
important. I think he feels like he sort of missed out, like he wanted to do
more volunteer or social work or something. So, he's happy for me."

Seeking His Niche

Matt went into his first year of teaching with the idea that he wanted
to get kids excited about nature and expose them to new experiences
outdoors. He explained that he wanted to "get kids into the environment,
get them turned on to it, get them excited about science, get them interested in stewardship." Whenever possible, he took his students on informal outings to the stream across the street and volunteered to take small
groups on bird-watching and hiking excursions on the weekends. However, Matt faced a difficult road during his first two years in the classroom. First, he struggled to establish a positive classroom climate, noting
that his primary purpose now was simply, "respecting adults. You just
need to respect a teacher and don't talk when they're talking and stay in
your seat when you're asked and follow rules."

Also, he often felt that as a new teacher among more established educators, he had to fight for materials, field trip approval, and other resources for his students, noting, "I was at the bottom of the totem pole. I was the new environmental science teacher. I was the youngest in age and I was kind of pushed aside a lot. I tried to do field trips and they nipped it in the bud before it started." Moreover, Matt faced a difficult year personally, suffering unexplained medical problems coupled with a breakup from a longtime girlfriend while still in the hospital. Although he was encouraged to quit teaching after his health difficulties to reduce his stress level, Matt stuck with it, in large part so that he did not let his father down. Matt said, "I didn't want to disappoint my dad. You know, don't quit, don't be a quitter, that kind of thing. It's kind of like, I'm going to show them I can do this. Because of the way I was raised, failure wasn't an option really."

After two years at his initial school, Matt decided to attend a transfer fair within the district and moved down the street to another city school. Now in his third year of teaching, Matt was a more seasoned educator who established positive student relationships and began informally mentoring newer teachers at the school. He felt that he could finally be himself in the classroom, describing, "I don't raise my voice. I'm a laid-back person, and I can be a laid-back teacher." He was pleased with the stronger support network, noting the active parent-teacher association and commenting, "I'm right down the street, but yet night and day. When I call parents it's just like, oh, thank you so much for calling."

And Matt respected the school leadership, noting, "The principal is more supportive. Like how it [was] always the teacher's fault over there. Here it's more supportive." Matt at times even saw himself as a liaison between the faculty and the administration, voicing support for his school during staff happy hours and other social events: "I've been a supporter of the administration so often, like guys, why are you focusing on the negative? Trust me, this is one of the best schools I've been to." At this school, Matt began to think about his own growth as a professional, envisioning a teacher leader or department chair role somewhere in his future.

During this time, Matt also threw himself with a passion into creating environmental experiences for his students. He wrote a number of grants, organized field trips, attended an environmental education conference, and gathered free resources for his students wherever he could get them. He willingly shared his materials and plans with fellow environmental science teachers, particularly those just starting out. And this time around, his efforts were supported by the administration. He explained, "Every field trip I've asked for, I've gotten. Every one."

Perhaps his greatest accomplishment in this realm was the new school garden. Matt wrote a grant and was awarded $2,000 to construct the garden in a field adjacent to the building. Although he ran up against some resistance from the school's athletic director, who considered the land to be part of her playing fields, in general the garden was a great success. Matt secured tree donations, compost, gardening tools, and more from local organizations, and envisioned expanding the garden into a neighborhood environmental center, open to the local community. "This thing just keeps getting bigger and bigger," he noted. Also, Matt's principal appreciated his efforts, commenting, "I can really see a difference in your kids than the environmental science kids last year."

During that same year, Matt also took on the job of tennis coach and introduced many of his students to the sport for the first time. Matt arranged for transportation to nearby tennis courts and taught his students the skills of the game. He was extremely pleased with his ability to connect with students through tennis, forming such strong bonds with some individuals that he was invited to their homes for dinner. Matt explained, "Something is working here. And I'd thought that was going to happen. That's why I was interested in teaching. Because I was hoping that what happened when I was a camp counselor was going to take place when I was a teacher." He also noticed a difference in his students after being on the court: "just the way they walk down the halls." By the end of the season, although it was their first year playing tennis, Matt's boys doubles placed second in the city. "Tennis keeps me going," he said. "It's what brings me to school some days. I'm so proud of that team. If I leave William City tomorrow, that would be the thing I'm most proud of."

Matt's efforts both within and outside of the classroom were recognized at his school. He was asked to teach an environmental research elective the following year and sponsor the Student Government Association. He was awarded Teacher of the Year. Matt noted, "It just feels good to be appreciated. It makes you want to come out here on the weekends and after school, when you're not getting paid, and work on the garden. I felt good about what I was doing, and they noticed, they encouraged." But his dedication to his work was beginning to wear away at his personal life, impacting his relationship with a new girlfriend, Kara, a fellow William City teacher. "I'm putting out a lot of energy and it's affecting my personal life a bit. I mean, Kara and I are getting along very well, but she wants me to be there and not talk about school. And they're e-mailing me all day long. They call me. Sometimes until 10:30 at night I'm doing stuff." Despite his great successes, Matt was beginning to feel a little burned out.

Moving Out of Urban Schools

Things began to go precipitously downhill during his fourth year in the classroom. First, Matt's school was moved into a different building, resulting in the loss of his schoolyard garden. Second, two of his best tennis players transferred out of the school, an experience that Matt described as having "the wind knocked out of me." Third, a rise in gang activity in the community gave him the sense that the school administration was losing control of the building. "I don't feel like the administration has control of their kids, and they have no solutions," he said. "The gangs, the Bloods are getting through here and recruiting. We have kids in here that don't go to class. All they do is keep getting in trouble where the police are running after them, arresting them, and they just come right back and they're in. We can't get rid of them. Just give us a solution." Together, these problems began to give Matt a feeling of hopelessness about the difficulties of educating children living in poverty. He said:

> The school system in general just seems like it's going to fail. It's so frustrating. I feel like you have to change the whole William City culture. The kids that are messed up and the family structure isn't there, parents aren't reading to their kids and not helping them with their homework and not holding them accountable for anything. How can you change that? I don't think the schools can change that, not anytime soon.

Although he remained committed, particularly to his after-school endeavors with students, Matt decided that it was time to move out of the city schools, saying, "I have to be done. Until they get control over the school, I just can't get through."

In the end, the day-to-day grind became too much for Matt. He explained that he was "constantly battling little things," particularly student behavior. "I'm tired of enforcing basic rules all the time. Why do I feel so drained and feel like I'm not living life to its fullest? I just need to do something different." Matt explained his reasons for leaving:

> You know, if I was changing everybody's lives, that's different. But to go through all that punishment just to have a couple of kids want to talk about tennis or SGA or enjoying an organization I started, it's not enough. The pain you go through all year long, the abuse you take during the day and then not having a nine-to-five job when you go home and you're just continually thinking about this place–that's not a positive place. It's not worth it. I could die tomorrow. I could die next year. This isn't living life. We count down the days until weekends. We count down the days until holidays. We count down the months until summer vacation.

On top of these feelings of frustration, Matt also began to feel that the stress of working in a high-poverty environment was changing who he was, saying, "I didn't become the person I wanted to be." On another occasion he noted, "I felt like I was changing as a person. I was just more angry or depressed or just pessimistic about education."

These factors came together during his fourth year of teaching and convinced Matt that the time had come to try something new. His girlfriend was also ready to leave urban teaching and together they began considering their options for next steps, including moving out west or internationally, noting, "We're young. We don't have any kids. We don't have any family here." Matt in particular talked about wanting to pursue his passion for exposing children to nature, commenting, "I want to do something special for kids. I don't know how I'm going to do it. I'm always thinking about doing something memorable, where the kids will always remember it. Taking kids hiking for a month, you know. Just getting them out of their environment, having counselors there to talk about stuff and having them open their eyes to nature and the power behind it." Moreover, Matt felt drained and was looking for a job that would energize and excite him. He explained, "I used to have all this energy. I want a job where I get energy. And that's what it is. People take energy; people give you energy. And it's taking my energy."

Although they dreamed of moving west or exploring other career paths, Matt and Kara had recently purchased a home in the suburbs of William City. They recognized that, with a new mortgage, the most sensible thing was to secure new teaching jobs in the local area. Matt commented, "Why did we do it? Now we're stuck. So we'll probably stay in the area because of that. We're not happy about it, but we have vacations." Given the situation, Matt decided to attend a career fair for a neighboring, suburban school district with a more affluent student population. He was offered two new jobs, both in biology, and ultimately accepted a position at a large high school with a well-regarded athletic program and an air-conditioned building. Plus, he said, "the neighborhood seemed nice" and the high school "looked like" the one he himself attended in the United States. His girlfriend also moved to a new elementary school close to their home.

Even though it was his fifth year of teaching, Matt was anxious about switching to a new school environment, noting, "I'm going from the city where I teach at a certain level, and have certain types of assignments, and now I'm sure it's going to be at a higher standard. Am I going to be a first-year teacher again? And I came here and I felt like I sort of was." In addition to developing new lesson plans for biology, Matt felt that the types of classroom management strategies he used with his urban students were not effective in this new environment. Previously, he felt that he had to be "mean and nasty" to keep control, whereas in the new school teacher-student discourse was generally more respectful.

Finding His Niche, Again

Although Matt quickly became accustomed to the practices at his new school, it took several years before he felt at ease with his new colleagues and administration. First, the environment was far less collaborative than at his old school, where many teachers were novices working together to learn how to teach. At his new school, most teachers had families and did not have time for social events after school hours. He explained that in the city, "we were all struggling. And so you're going through a lot of tough times, and it brings you together. You're a support system. Out here, at a better school, there isn't a lot of that." Second, shortly after he arrived the department chair was forced to lay off a science teacher because of declining student enrollment. As Matt was the most recent to arrive, he fully expected that person to be him and was surprised to discover that it was instead one of his more senior colleagues. Although relieved to have kept his job, Matt felt that many in the department resented his presence there, commenting, "She was a good teacher. People got really upset. And from that point, I guess I never really felt accepted."

Finally, Matt felt that he was in many ways "hazed" by his department chair and school administration. In lesson observation after observation, Matt received low scores, despite always running his plans by the department chair and taking all of the advice offered. The situation finally came to a head during his final evaluation before tenure, when Matt was once again poised to earn a "needs improvement," jeopardizing his chance at tenure. Feeling he had nothing to lose, Matt decided to confront the situation. He recalled his words to the school principal and department chair:

> Before you tell me what's going on, I need to talk. Every time I come in here, I get this negativity. I don't feel supported. It's just, "You didn't do this, you didn't do that." It's never, "You did this really well." I know I have some strengths here. I know it. I feel it. I feel like I'm between a rock and a hard place here. If you guys want to get rid of me, you should have done it way back. And if you're thinking it now, then definitely get rid of me. But before I go, please tell me, I feel like my kids did so well on the [biology exam]. Can you please at least give me the scores of my kids on their [exams]?

It turned out that Matt's students had earned the highest scores in the school on their standardized exam. Armed with that information, Matt was able to negotiate a more positive evaluation and ultimately secure tenure in his new district. Shortly after the incident, Matt's department chair retired and a new leader came on who treated Matt in a more professional manner, securing him a more flexible schedule and ultimately his own classroom, so that he did not have to float from room to room.

Despite these challenges, Matt found great success with his students both academically and personally. In addition to helping them regularly earn among the highest biology test scores in the school, he also formed a strong bond with many students, whose birthday cards, class photos, and other tokens of affection now line his classroom walls. One former student, now in college to become an English teacher, even wrote a poem about Matt. Matt said it was "about my impact on his life. It brought a tear to my eye, actually." But perhaps the most meaningful interaction with students came, once again, through tennis.

For the first two years, Matt continued to commute back into the city to coach at his old school. But when the students he started with graduated and the coaching position opened up at his current school, Matt took the job. He worked to make the tennis team a more serious enterprise, noting, "I just made it much more competitive. Kids on the first day were wearing jeans and boots. So I just made it much more strict and structured. I have Saturday practices. We were going out to [the local] community college where there was ten or twelve courts and I had them all out there playing these challenge matches and tournaments. It was cool." By his second year as coach, they were one of the top teams in the district, with one girls doubles team competing at the state level. Matt also worked with a local recreation center to start a winter tennis season so that many of his students could practice year-round.

Now five years into teaching in a suburban environment, and nine years into the profession, Matt was relatively settled in his current job. He and Kara were planning a wedding as well as a family in the near future. They spent six weeks in Hawaii over last summer's break, taking full advantage of their teaching schedules. And he felt comfortable in his job, noting, "It's a lot easier, and I need that right now. I feel like I need a job where I don't have to think, where I don't have to multitask all the time." However, Matt was still not fully satisfied with his career. He explained, "I wanted to work with inner-city youth and I thought that was going to be my niche in life. Where I was going to make a difference. When I realized I wasn't and now I'm here, I was kind of like, What am I doing? I didn't get into teaching to teach. The whole reason I got into this has been all unraveled and now I'm not here for any of the reasons why." In many ways, Matt felt that the teaching profession was not what he originally envisioned, noting, "the teaching job, in general I feel like on paper, it just seems so great," but has perhaps failed to live up to his expectations.

Continuing to Explore

What Matt really wanted to do was get kids excited about science and nature. However, with the pressure of the state exam he rarely took his students outdoors anymore, except during a few weeks at the end of the year once testing has been completed. He did not feel that the emphasis on standardized testing was the way to spark interest in science, joking, "Yeah, you want to learn science. Well, here is a test. You like science, well, memorize this!" Although he had been quite successful in preparing students for the exam, he found himself getting sucked into a testing culture that he did not truly believe in. He explained:

> I hate it because I'm so focused on the damn test scores. And I'm like, this isn't important, Matt. What are you doing? What have you come to? It's funny. When I was in the city, it was kind of like I'm becoming someone I don't want to be, and now here I am, again, becoming someone I don't want to be. When am I going to be able to teach the way I want to teach? Maybe I'm not going to. My cup is not 100 percent filled in a public school in the United States.

But it was not only the testing culture that Matt found disappointing. It was also the students' indifference to learning. He noted, "I just want to see kids excited about learning, and I thought they would be out here, and they're not. They're just very apathetic and it sucks me dry."

From time to time, Matt questioned his career choice and wondered, "Looking back, am I going to be like, what did I accomplish? I'm looking at my job and I'm thinking, am I going to really be proud of what I'm doing? And I think the answer is no." Disappointed that the structure of school failed to inspire passion for science and nature, Matt considered other options, including a naturalist position with the district. He wondered if he should take a more active role in shaping his future career, noting, "I'm trying to go where the wind takes me. Maybe I need to start grabbing the ropes of the sailboat and going in some direction." Although he thought about moving to another job, an active job search was only in his mind because, in the end, "a job is just a job. Something sounds great, but. . . . " For now Matt resolved to focus on tennis, his relationships with students, and the other aspects of his work that he found most satisfying.

RAYA

The most senior of the eight case study teachers, Raya is currently in her fifties and dresses with an artistic flair. She left a successful career in science communication to try teaching nine years ago, in what she saw as her version of the "Peace Corps," an opportunity to contribute to a community in need. Raya grew up in a military family and moved every two to three years to bases around the United States and Germany. Her mother, a dedicated homemaker, worked hard to provide a "very rich, stimulating environment" for the children, with art around the home and countless enriching experiences. She also fostered her children's interests whenever possible. Raya noted, "I was really into oceanography. And so, she would buy us books, and we would go to aquariums whenever we traveled. She would basically support whatever interests the kids had in their minds."

Raya's mother was also a staunch advocate of public education, always enrolling her children in base schools or the local public schools. In one instance, Raya and her siblings arrived to discover that they were among a handful of White children in a rural southern school. She explained, "We'd been at the school before it was integrated. And we were shipped from there to Germany. When we came back, we went from Germany to Texas to Idaho, and when we came back to South Carolina, they'd integrated the schools and most of the White people went to private schools. And so the schools were primarily Black."

After spending her middle school years at this school, Raya moved with her family to southern California, where she attended a "very nice, but overcrowded" high school with upwards of 2,500 students. Raya thrived there, participating in the athletic, choral, and drama programs, but felt that the large class sizes prevented her from developing writing and other academic skills in any meaningful way. She explained, "I was mostly in honors classes and basically coasted on my verbal skills. I never learned to write in school, mostly because they were moving a lot of kids through. I never created a project. I never had to write any significant paper. I never had any of those skills. But I graduated at the top of my class."

After high school, Raya enrolled in a northeastern liberal arts college but arrived to discover that her academic skills were far below those of her peers, many of whom had attended private prep schools. She struggled initially, noting, "I really worked my first six months at [college], I worked really hard because I wanted good grades, and I didn't have the skills I needed to get the grades I wanted. I asked around and really worked hard to do the sort of skill building I needed." Although she ultimately gained the academic skills she needed to be successful in college, Raya remained unhappy in this small, insular environment and decided to transfer back to a large public university in southern California. There, she majored in marine biology and worked with a local research institute on fish collection.

Exploring Scientific Communications

Immediately after college, Raya joined the Merchant Marines and served for a year and a half on a ship, first doing sampling as part of the science crew and later working in the engine room as part of the engineering crew. Frequently the only woman aboard the ship, working in what she termed, "nasty ocean conditions," Raya nonetheless enjoyed her work, commenting, "I loved it, I loved it. I puked my guts out. I loved it so much." From the Merchant Marines, Raya returned to graduate school and earned a master's in science communication, where she "learned to write out of necessity, writing thousands and thousands of stories for newspapers." She then held a series of communications jobs, from reporter for small local newspapers to director of communications for college campuses. As she progressed in her career, Raya moved back east and produced interactive media for broadcasting companies. Throughout all of these jobs, Raya maintained the common thread of interpreting science, explaining, "It's all informal science education in one way or another. I've always done some sort of translation in writing, interactive media, the web."

Choosing Urban Teaching

While working toward a master's in instructional technology as part of her job at a national broadcasting company, and living in William City, Raya was exposed for the first time to nontraditional models for education. She said:

> You talked about project-based learning and student-centered learning, and constructive authority. I said, oh my goodness, this is so cool. This is nothing I had when I was growing up. But this would be really fun because I've always been a project manager, a facilitator, and that's exactly what you do in the classes. You set it up and then you help everybody figure out how to do it. This will be really fun.

Inspired by these educational approaches and feeling that she had "gotten to a place in my career where I wasn't completely satisfied," Raya decided to try out urban teaching. She explained:

> It was a combination of having done this master's work and seeing how cool it could be and how creative, because it's really important for me to have a creative job. And also it was time for me in my life to give back to the community. I've had a very rich career, and I've been able to travel a lot, and I've been very successful on many different levels, and it was kind of like, it's time. It's time to do this, and William City would be the place to do that. I very much am charmed by the city.

After doing her homework by reading about urban education and observing in several local classrooms, Raya decided to enroll in an urban teacher education program, where her master's was paid for if she made the commitment to teach in William City for five years. She planned to teach the five required years and then reevaluate, noting, "I have to reassess in five years. I have to reassess where William City is. I have to reassess where I am as a teacher."

Raya entered teaching in her mid-forties, coming into the profession as a career changer. In many ways, it was an unusual move for her, as she had never wanted to be a teacher. Growing up, she described her teachers as "goofy" and noted, "I was never interested in becoming a teacher because they were really boring people. They weren't very interesting to me." However, although Raya did not think she would have been a successful educator immediately out of college, she now felt that she brought a wealth of life experience to the classroom that aided in her effectiveness. Raya explained that in urban education in particular:

> I think it really takes a certain amount of stamina, and I think it really helps if you're older and you have a firmer grip on who you are. You know, I really try to imagine what it would be like to go into that right out of college. I think that very few people have life experiences enough to be able to cope with the intensity of the experience in a really productive, solid way. You have to be just really tough. And I think it's really hard to have that toughness just coming out of school. You have more perspective as you're getting older in terms of being able to do a professional distance thing that allows you to be effective. You know, and you're not out to save the world.

Raya also struggled with the transition into teaching because it constituted a 50 percent pay cut from her previous position. Disappointed that the pay scale only accounted for years of teaching, rather than other relevant organizational and interpersonal skills, Raya resolved to "figure out financially how to do this. It gets very tight. I've had to cut back on a lot of stuff, and I'm very bare bones. I used to travel a lot, and now I have to be very careful." Whereas she used to have a gym membership, cable television, and make substantial donations to charity, now as a teacher, "All my donations go to my classroom."

When Raya decided to go into teaching, she had a clear commitment to working with a high-need student population. She noted, "I wouldn't teach in just a regular suburban classroom because I didn't go into teaching to do that. That doesn't interest me. I'm pretty much committed to the population that I teach." In addition, Raya remained exclusively focused on making her contribution in the classroom. She rejected numerous opportunities to move out of classroom teaching and into educational leadership positions, which she considered to be bureaucratic work.

Raya explained, "People ask me often if that's what I'm interested in, but I've already done all that. I've already been the leader in different organizations. So you know, I'm really interested in the trench work and working with the students. What I want to do right now is become a really good teacher." Although she initially took a leadership role in her grade-level team, she made a concerted effort to mentor other teachers so they would soon be able to take over the responsibility, noting, "I have people wanting to pull me into administrative stuff, and I just tell them no. They want me to facilitate meetings, they want me to do professional development, and I'm like, I don't want to be principal. I know how to do this stuff already. I don't need the experience."

At the same time, Raya came into the classroom with what she described as a "good compass" about where she was headed with students, working to develop them as lifelong learners and problem solvers. She described her approach: "My bottom line goal overall is to give my kids the skills to be lifelong learners. So they know how to research a problem, to ask questions about a problem, and get information to help solve the problem. You know that they know, if they have a problem, that they're not helpless. They know how to go about solving it. So it's an attitude and a skill base."

In addition to this overarching goal, Raya also worked in a concerted way on particular academic skills. Literacy was a priority for her because, "their writing skills and their attitudes about writing are so low." Integrating math skills into science was also essential. In addition, Raya decried what she considered the "arrogance" of the science curriculum and focused narrowly on what she viewed as important and relevant understandings in science, noting, "I want them to be able to understand everyday science. I want them to know that trees are living things. I want them to know where they get their food from. I want them to understand the relationships, how things are connected."

Learning to Operate in the School Context

Although Raya had a clear vision for her role and purpose in the classroom, when she first began teaching at a newly restructured high school in William City, she nevertheless struggled as she became accustomed to working with students from impoverished communities. She used a process of trial and error to determine what worked in the classroom, explaining:

> I tried several different things. I was getting a sense of where my kids were as a new teacher, and I basically was overshooting every time what they were capable of doing. So I sort of had to keep ratcheting down. I had to learn how to better structure things so that my kids could pick it up in bits and pieces because they were really having a hard time with what I thought was pretty simple.

Over time, she learned to break skills and content into bite-sized chunks, noting, "What I've learned is I have to take it in baby steps and get them started and have them have more and more successful experiences, go in with a very focused goal in mind. [My first year] was really revelatory for me in trying to figure out where my kids were and where I needed to have my instruction be for them." By her third year in the classroom, Raya had a much better sense of where her students were starting, explaining, "I feel like I've gotten a handle on my classes in terms of getting them focused much faster this year. So I'm driving them at a harder, faster pace this year."

When she first began, Raya was also dismayed by the utter lack of resources available to her for teaching in general, and teaching science in particular, noting, "You have to beg, borrow, and steal to get computers." She was surprised how little was available even to supply her classroom, explaining, "I think I was just really shocked at how little there was in terms of what I would consider basic professional equipment support. I think I was just shocked that you had to scramble for an overhead. I have a very ghetto screen. You know, things that are really fundamental to what you do, you have to really scratch for." She noted that English and math were tested subjects, so those teachers were given supplies from the district, whereas in science, "any new materials were from grants, or from out of my pocket. It would be really nice to rely on a regular pocket of money that I could spend, and not have to go through the [district office] and get lost in whatever convolutions are there. It would be really nice to have supplies every year."

In an effort to offer meaningful learning experiences for her students in a resource-limited environment, Raya took advantage of numerous opportunities available to teachers in the local community, bringing in speakers, writing grants, and partnering with nonprofits and universities whenever possible. She explained, "I spend a lot of time building part-nerships with community members: All of that brings in experts and resources and projects for my students. So I have to be active in the community to deal with those connections for my kids so they can see things in their neighborhoods and how their work in class connects with their real lives." In an effort to establish and sustain relationships in the local community, Raya dedicated numerous personal hours to serving on boards of local environmental organizations, participating in professional development workshops, and conducting classroom research.

In her instruction, Raya was attracted to a project-based approach, saying, "I'm just an active learner and generally interested in projects." She encouraged her principal to adopt the same curriculum model school-wide. The approach used questions to guide learning in thematic units. Raya described the model: "The whole idea is that you're teaching students accountability and ownership, and there's sort of character in-struction, as well as content instruction. And so on a daily basis, you should see in all the classrooms a lot of student work; you should see active engagement from students in talking about community and their roles in the community." Through this model, Raya developed a number of thematic units centered on authentic questions, such as, "How does the environment affect temperature, the urban heat island effect?" She con-ducted these question-driven lessons in the park surrounding her school building as well as on numerous trips to local nature preserves and other sites.

With students, Raya adopted a highly professional and no-nonsense approach with the idea that it was part of her job to help students deal with the challenges that inevitably arose in their lives. She explained her reasoning:

Part of it is the kids have to learn not to live in a drama culture. You can't be in drama all the time; you won't make it through school, you won't make it through college, and you certainly won't make it through work if you are not in control of understanding how to deal with these situations. You can't always control the situations, but you can control how you respond to them. And you've got to learn some coping skills that help sort of modulate your behavior.

Raya felt this professional approach also sustained her over the long term, preventing her from burning out by getting too involved in students' personal lives. She commented:

I don't take that on. I think there is a lot of wear and tear on teachers because they do take it on, and they're not trained or equipped to do that. And I think that I'm in it for the long haul. I'm sort of an endurance runner, and I can't go on too many sprints because otherwise I won't last, and I won't do anybody any good. So I believe my job is to be very stable and consistent and supportive, and not be pulled off track or used. I have to draw a line. I just try and keep it professional.

With this perspective, Raya constructed a highly professional classroom environment focused on concrete academic skills, where personal crisis was not welcome. She explained, "I try to be approachable if something's wrong. If you need help with your drama, I'll find you someone, but I'm not doing your drama here."

Building Relationships with Colleagues

Beyond the classroom, Raya was frustrated by many of her interactions with administrators and fellow teachers. Her first year, in particular, she had a rocky relationship with her school principal, who Raya considered threatened by her independence and professionalism. She explained:

I almost quit my first year because of her. She's very threatened by me. I came in from the corporate world. She's only been in education. And I'm used to participating in an organization. And I expect other people to treat me professionally, and I treat them professionally. But in the inner-city, traditionally, it's been very hierarchical, very punitive, very dictatorial, and that was how she was raised and that was her initial reaction. And she came down very hard on me, which is really hard on a first year teacher.

By her second year, however, Raya felt her principal began to recognize her as an asset to the school and no longer worried that Raya was after her job. From that point, their relationship improved dramatically and Raya served on several leadership committees to support the school and students.

Despite the improvement in her relationship with her administrator, Raya remained disappointed by her interactions with colleagues, noting, "Teachers are weird. That's all I can say. They are just plain weird. They have all sorts of insecurities." In particular, Raya felt that her fellow educators lacked the professional skills needed to work together as a team, explaining, "I find teachers the most unprofessional people I've ever met, and I haven't quite figured out why. But they have a really hard time being what I consider professional, which is sort of showing up to meetings on time and talking about what's going on, being productive." Moreover, she simply did not find most of them to be pleasant companions, noting, "I just don't like very many of my colleagues. I don't. It's not very much fun working with them."

Although she considered some of the newer teachers in her building, particularly the Teach for America corps members, to be very interesting people, she nevertheless avoided spending too much time supporting her more novice colleagues, preferring instead to dedicate herself to her own classroom and students. She explained:

> They have a lot of questions, everything from classroom management to equipment, which we don't have much of, to basically how things work, the day-to-day operations of the school. And then just wanting to talk. This is the most stressful, and I don't let it happen very much. On top of everything I do because we work in such a stressful environment with such demanding students. You know things happen all the time and then the teachers have to process it. I don't allow that at school because I can't pick that up on some of my own stuff. I've got my own kids that I'm dealing with.

Although Raya did for some time maintain a blog with practical suggestions for new urban teachers, she intentionally steered clear of becoming a key support person for the seemingly endless stream of new teachers who entered her building.

Finding Her Way to Make a Difference

Raya remained the environmental studies teacher at this high school for four years, but by the middle of her fourth year she was beginning to feel drained. For one, her class sizes had ballooned to over thirty students. She noted, "It's the emotional, physical demand in managing a class of thirty kids. Keeping kids in line is really a handful." Second, her student population was increasingly demanding, with large numbers of students who had learning as well as emotional difficulties. Raya explained, "We had 30 percent IEPs in our school, most of them male, most of them just having a hard time staying seated. We had such a high IEP population, or classes where we had three students who are classified as mentally retarded, and three students who are identified as emotionally disturbed." She felt incapable of meeting these intense student needs without outside support. Third, Raya still struggled to maintain a sustainable work-life balance. She was working long hours, arriving at school around 7:00 in the morning, staying late into the evening, and planning her classes each weekend. According to Raya, this lifestyle was making her "tired and borderline depressed. I was wearing out." Altogether, Raya felt that she was constantly under stress. She noted, "It's like being in the emergency room all the time. I can't let down for a day."

Beyond this personal stress, Raya also began to lose confidence in her ability to enact change within the confines of her classroom. She felt there was only so much she could accomplish within what she termed a "broken system," which lacked community, staff, and administrator stability. She explained, "It's bigger than me. I feel like I'm doing everything that I'm able to do within my classroom. But making change requires more than just what is going on in your classroom." Raya also felt that the larger circumstances of the neighborhood schools, with their transient student population and high levels of acting out, prevented her from making the difference she had hoped for:

> When you're teaching, you want to feel like you're making a difference. And I do think I've been making a difference for a number of students, but there are a number of students that I think are checked out, and there's nothing I can do right now because I just have too much on my plate. It's frustrating to feel like you could do more if it was a better circumstance.

In her fourth year, Raya decided it was time to move on, noting, "I would love to stay with my school, but I won't get beaten up like I am this year. It's just too stressful."

Frustrated with her current environment, Raya nevertheless felt that she had only just become a fully competent educator. She explained that in teaching, "You take the first two years, and then it's your turn to give." Wanting to stay in the classroom until she had the opportunity to give back in meaningful ways, Raya resolved to remain in teaching for a little while longer. She explained, "I'd like to teach a few years more. I think I finally have my chops and I'd like to keep doing that for a while, but only if I can call the shots of what it looks like." Rejecting a move to the suburbs because of its scripted curriculum and more privileged student population, Raya instead accepted a position as a sixth-, seventh-, and eighth-grade science teacher at a small and stable K-8 charter school with an economically integrated student body. Although this move entailed a substantial amount of work rewriting her curriculum for both subject areas and grade levels, Raya accepted the challenge.

Moving Again

Raya stayed at this charter school for three school years, rotating between life, physical, and environmental sciences each year and revising her curriculum accordingly. During this time, she continued her work building strong relationships with community partners, earning grants, and developing her content expertise. This school also allowed her to "see the full extent of capabilities for those ages. Because I had doctors' daughters and I had kids who were in more perilous situations, I was able to say, okay, this is what a competent sixth-grader can do. I could see within each grade level the spectrum. That helped me orient in terms of the possibilities."

However, Raya struggled with a controlling principal who did not grant her the independence she wanted in the classroom. Raya said, "I started head-butting with the principal because she was very intimidated. I was very successful at bringing in grants. I was very successful at field trips. I had very clear ideas and I said them. I think she decided it was difficult for teachers to have autonomy." After some time, the principal stopped signing her grants or approving her field trips, perhaps out of a concern about jealousy from colleagues. "She shut me down," Raya lamented. Ultimately, Raya decided that she needed to look around once more for an environment where she could maintain her independence. Raya moved for the second time to an operator school, run by a group that had a network of schools in William City and neighboring locations.

At this school, she taught sixth-grade earth science, yet another new subject for Raya to master. The transitions took their toll on her personal life because, as Raya notes, "I'm always designing [curriculum] over and over and over again." However, despite the continuous changes, Raya was relatively pleased with her new school context. For one, Raya enjoyed teaching sixth grade because she felt that it was where, "the rubber hits the road" in terms of developing important academic skills and study habits for later school success.

In addition, her new school promoted a high level of teacher autonomy and collaboration. For two years, Raya worked closely with a team of fellow teachers to design schedules, coordinate progress reports, and support student learning. And Raya enjoyed and respected her colleagues at this school, whom she described as a "nice mix" of novice and more veteran educators, with a large proportion of male teachers. Raya explained, "It's a very committed, smart, hard-working group. This is an everyone-pulls-their-weight group. And our team is pretty strong in terms of sitting on the sixth-graders and working them all the time."

Raya saw all members of her team as contributing in unique ways, based on their strengths. Her particular role was to facilitate grants and field trips and mentor her more novice colleagues in these processes. Now allowed to stretch her wings, Raya coordinated numerous projects, including a weeklong outdoor education camp, several local field trips, a science fair, a reader's corner, guest classroom scientists, and an initiative to turn one quarter of the parking lot into a school garden. Although she still rejected a move into school administration, Raya began to mentor many of her younger colleagues in order to build their capacity. In one example Raya explained, "Last year I organized all of the [outdoor education camps] and this year I decentralized it. So I coached all the homerooms on how to do it."

Still Exploring

In addition, although Raya completed her ninth year in the classroom, she continued to grow as an educator. She devoted herself to building her expertise in earth science, spending over three weeks of her summer and several weekends in academies to develop content knowledge and effective approaches for teaching it. She also continually adjusted her instructional methods, moving over time from a strictly project-based approach to one that more explicitly teaches standards-based content and basic skills using a variety of interactive methods. According to Raya, "I focus on the standards and I just do it in different ways over, and over, and over again, so that they finally get the whole vocabulary and finally get the concept." While dubbing her students "earth science investigators," she simultaneously zeroed in on what she considers to be the most critical literacy skills, "note taking, reading different texts, learning different graphic organizers for comparing and contrasting, key details."

Although Raya considered her school to be the best available working conditions in the city, she was still undecided about staying there long-term. Primarily, a decision by the school's administration to add two extra remediation classes on top of the core curriculum had her run down and exhausted. She explained:

> I'm a grouchy teacher this year. I'm a grouchy teacher because I'm just getting through. I'm so tired with everything that has to be done: all the additional role with additional classes, the management of the grades in the additional classes, and then filling the time so that it's somehow engaging and meaningful. It's just been really hard when really what I wanted to do was apply all these things I've been learning. That makes the work richer.

Her experience this past year raised the question once again of moving on. Raya asked herself, "Is this where I want to be or do I need to go? Do I need to leave the city because it won't get better than what I have? That was a real serious consideration." At the current moment, Raya decided to stay in her position for one more year. However, if her schedule does not ease up, she resolved to look for something new the following year.

Raya originally planned to stay in teaching for only five years, and did consider moving out of the classroom and into other fields, such as "the interface between communications, urban education, and science." However, after talking with several contacts, she learned that it would be difficult to transition at this point specifically because of her age. She explained:

> I have to [stay in teaching] because of my age. I think it's really difficult to transition in your fifties. I had thought I would maybe teach five years, this was my Peace Corps, and then I would move out. Then the economy shifted and I was still challenged. I found it interesting. But I'm finding now that as I'm looking at positions it's really difficult for people my age to transition out because they can find someone who is younger and who is willing to work for less money.

Faced with the reality of ending her career in teaching, Raya noted, "It's been really difficult actually. You find you sort of hit a wall."

Undaunted, Raya contemplated a move from William City into a neighboring suburban school district. Although she was originally opposed to this type of teaching context, recent experiences in professional development workshops put her into contact with some exceptional teachers from local districts. She met one teacher, in particular, who amazed Raya with her ability to communicate the meaning of scientific variables to students. Raya explained, "She's the one who I learned how to break down variables from. She's the one person I've ever seen who has been able to do this. That's the first time I'd actually ever seen anybody really model open-ended inquiry so that it was meaningful and I was able to say, okay, now I can adapt that and do it with my kids. That was huge." Inspired by this teacher, Raya decided to explore this possible connection if conditions do not improve at her school the following year. In the meantime, she enjoyed traveling across the Unites States as well as to Greece and Australia with a new boyfriend and remained a committed and professional classroom educator.

THEMES

We can learn a considerable amount about teachers' career trajectories not only from shifters and leavers, but from stayers as well. Sonia Nieto (2001), in her work with veteran urban teachers, found four features that "keep teachers going" over time, including their own autobiographies, their students, their visions for reform, and their engagement in the intellectual craft of teaching. While these three case study teachers were not yet veterans, their experiences did in many ways mirror those from Nieto's work by following their initial intentions, connecting with students and schooling in ways they found meaningful, and continually growing over time. Moreover, while these teachers were in their seventh to ninth years in the classroom, they were very much veterans at their school sites, already taking on both formal and informal leadership roles. This echoes Ingersoll and Merrill's (2012) reflection that today's urban schools are largely staffed by young and inexperienced teachers, such that those with even a few years of teaching under their belt become early veterans.

Theme #1: Stayers Adjusted Their Approaches in Order to Thrive

One important theme that cuts across the experiences of Denise, Matt, and Raya, echoing Nieto's framework, is the notion that these stayers searched for and eventually identified some aspect of their professional lives in which they could thrive. These teachers faced no-less-challenging workplace contexts than others who chose to shift or leave, but they managed those demands in particular ways. Overall, when one aspect of their professional lives did not go as planned, these teachers chose to continue searching for another manner by which they could make their contribution. For instance, Denise felt that she was making an impact through raising test scores and mentoring newer teachers, Matt found what he called his "niche" coaching tennis, and Raya focused on constructing field trips and other outdoor experiences for her students. What makes these educators unique among the case studies is that when challenges arose, they navigated around them within the system, rather than giving up on teaching or the field of education altogether.

Much has been written about the role of self-efficacy in contributing to teacher retention or attrition, with recent research indicating that beginning teachers have lower self-efficacy (Jensen, Sandoval-Hernandez, Knoll, & Gonzalez, 2012), that teachers with lower self-efficacy are more likely to leave the classroom (Johnson, Berg, & Donaldson, 2005), and that they are less satisfied with their jobs (Moe, Pazzaglia, & Ronconi, 2010). However, the experiences of these educators put self-efficacy into a different light. Rather than viewing self-efficacy as guiding teachers' career decisions, it seems that these teachers used their career intentions to shape their self-efficacy, finding new ways to feel successful professionally when the original goals did not work out as planned. While all three of these teachers certainly faced struggles in the classroom, they remained committed enough to teaching to reconstruct their professional priorities in ways that were better aligned with classroom realities and allowed them to thrive.

What these stayers considered to be a meaningful professional contribution seven or nine years into their careers was not always what they initially envisioned, although many of their underlying goals did remain consistent. However, the way they approached these goals frequently evolved over time. Denise at first was focused on developing mentoring relationships with students. However, as she grew older and felt more disconnected from the high school experience, she shifted her focus toward the mentoring of new teachers. Likewise, Matt initially hoped to expose his students to the outdoors. However, later in his career he found sports to be a more practical and generative way to broaden his students' horizons and build social as well as academic skills. Raya also shifted her focus from one particular project-based curricular model to a more eclectic approach that emphasized scientific and community-based partnerships.

What cuts across their experiences is the idea that these three stayers maintained the same underlying goals for their professional contribution, but adjusted their approaches based on contextual challenges and opportunities. Frustrations did not lead them to give up on education altogether, but rather to adjust their way of interacting within it.

Theme #2: Stayers Valued Their Contribution as Educators

Likewise, Denise, Matt, and Raya each held teaching, and their role in it, in high regard, seeing it as a worthwhile career for meeting their personal needs while simultaneously contributing to society. International reports (e.g., OECD, 2005, 2009) note that teaching is a profession in decline. However, teaching filled a valuable place in the lives of these three educators, each in its own way. Emerging out of her life experiences, Denise enjoyed teaching because it allowed her to mentor students like herself while also serving as a vehicle for social mobility into the middle class. Matt saw teaching as a stable and noble career that satisfied his family while grounding him in active and outdoor pursuits. And Raya saw teaching as a way to connect to her community and contribute to society in a way she had been unable to do in her previous career. Perhaps because these teachers so respected the work of teaching and saw it as integral to fulfilling personal, professional, and even societal needs, they remained committed to the classroom in one form or another.

Theme #3: Stayers Continually Explored Their Professional Options

Finally, the experiences of Denise, Matt, and Raya show us that exploration is not only present at the beginning of a career in teaching or at its end. Rather, exploration is an inherent part of a career in the classroom today. All three of these teachers seriously contemplated leaving teaching at one point or another. Denise considered leaving out of frustration during her early years and later to pursue teacher education. Matt thought about other routes for pursuing his passions, such as working in an outdoor school or as a teacher-naturalist. And Raya also briefly put out feelers for the possibility of blending her many skills in a new setting.

In addition to exploring career trajectories out of the classroom, all three likewise explored roles and responsibilities within education. Denise played many roles as a teacher and mentor, Matt sponsored student clubs from gardening to student government to badminton, and Raya continuously revised her curriculum while pursuing new partnerships. All three teachers also taught in more than one school setting as they sought out better working conditions. But one thing is clear: The teachers who remained in the classroom did not in any way lead static careers. Rather, they made the act of exploration an inherent part of their work lives as they constructed meaningful career trajectories within education.

FOUR

Those Who Shifted

I miss the kids a lot . . . but I was just totally worn out.
—Mitch, after shifting out of classroom teaching

A second set of teachers remained committed to working within the field of education. However, faced with unpleasant working conditions and inner-circle politics, these educators made the decision to shift out of classroom teaching and into educational leadership positions. When her mentor teacher role was eliminated, Alison decided to move from her school site to the district office and currently works with principals on improving school climate. However, when the right conditions come along, she would like to return to the schools as an assistant principal. Mitch explored both a magnet school and a charter school before leaving teaching, exhausted, for an educational nonprofit.

Although finding great success in his current role, he too would like to be more directly involved with schools and students. These educators are unique because of their enduring commitment to working with students, their resilience in the face of school politics, and their dynamic career paths within and outside of school sites. Their cases illustrate the ways that initial career motivations intersect with workplace contexts to shape career trajectories. They also highlight the importance of student and collegial relationships in what Goodson has called a center of gravity (Goodson, 1991) for teaching.

ALISON

An avid sports fan with a bubbly personality, Alison grew up in what she described as an upper-middle-class family in small towns across Pennsylvania and Maryland, where she explained, "The only thing between me and my best friend was a cornfield." She attended the public schools, which she described as "all White" and "very conservative." Alison thrived as an active and involved student leader, cheering on the school's sport teams, doing community service, and participating in an environmental student organization.

During high school, she became close with one biology teacher and worked as his student assistant for several years, scoring tests and helping him with paperwork. She also loved her chemistry teacher, who devoted eight full weeks to allowing students to identify a series of powered substances. Inspired by her interactions with these teachers as well as popular science-based movies and television shows, Alison decided she was interested in the sciences and "took all the science classes my school had to offer." She especially liked the physical sciences, where she could use clearly defined formulas to solve problems.

Choosing Teaching

During college Alison pursued the education track within her chemistry major and always kept the idea of teaching in the back of her mind, noting, "I always kind of thought in my head, 'I might want to teach,' 'oh, that would be fun to teach,' or 'when I'm a teacher' type of things in my head." She elected to stay on after graduation for a fifth year in order to earn her teaching certificate in chemistry, where she felt she had a strong teacher preparation experience. She explained that when she began in her own classroom, she felt more prepared than many of her peers: "Because I had already been in front of a class before, I had already been the teacher. I already had to write my own lesson plans . . . but I also got to do it while someone was helping me and guiding and coaching me." During her fifth-year certification program, Alison also became quite close with her science methods instructor, a former urban teacher who inspired her to use inquiry methods in the classroom. Alison explained, "She's always focusing on the inquiry-based and hands-on approach to things, just moving us so far away from the teacher-centered to much more student-centered approach." Alison continues to stay in touch with this instructor, explaining, "I still e-mail her, probably three or four times during the school year, usually if I have a question about something, or just to see how she's doing." This mentor continues to offer both instructional and professional support for Alison to this day.

In addition to influencing her pedagogy, this methods instructor also inspired Alison to teach in an urban context. Alison explained, "She taught in [urban] schools for a long time so I felt like she had knowledge to really tell me what it would be like to teach in the city system. She's always talking about how much she loved it, and after working with her, I knew that's what I wanted to do." At the conclusion of her certification program, Alison applied for jobs with several large, urban school systems up and down the East Coast. She was convinced she wanted to teach in a low-income community because her work would have greater influence. She explained, "I did my student teaching at a rich little White public school, and I knew that it's not what I wanted to do. I guess I just wanted to have a bigger impact, and I feel like I can have a bigger impact in the urban cities, [with] urban kids. I just feel like they don't have a lot of people who are interested in being there." Alison also explained that she loves the students: "They're just more genuine, more real as opposed to catered to and babied." After weighing offers from several school districts, Alison settled on William City because of a guaranteed contract.

Becoming an Essential Team Member

Alison's first year of teaching was in a large and unruly comprehensive high school, which the district divided into four smaller schools at the conclusion of the year. As a founding teacher in one of the restructured high schools, Alison became close with her principal, Dr. Jenkins, and several colleagues whom she described as the "core teachers" in the building. In addition to her full-time teaching responsibilities, Alison also helped out in countless ways across the school, leading 7:30 a.m. professional development sessions, writing the advisory curriculum, serving on the Student Support Team, participating in the Parent-Teacher Association, and aligning guidance folders, to name a few.

She also devoted the majority of her spring and summer breaks to helping with curriculum development and school improvement efforts, becoming the "go-to" teacher when her principal needed assistance. She found this work to be generally rewarding, noting, "I don't mind doing it. It needs to get done and I don't like when our school fails things." However, at times she expressed frustration with the "new kids" — that is, novice teachers who were not fully bought into school reform efforts. Reflecting back, Alison noted, "We had a lot of people who didn't buy into the culture of our school and the climate and our values. It's hard to let people in who don't buy into that." It is not surprising that Alison's efforts on behalf of the school earned her the award for "Best Team Player."

In addition to forging strong relationships with her school principal and a core group of colleagues, Alison's early years in the classroom were characterized by strong relationships with students. When asked about the most important aspects of her job as a teacher, Alison replied, "Talk to the kids on a little bit different level, about something that's happening at home or who they're living with now. Try and relate to my kids." The results of her emphasis on relationship building were evident in numerous ways, from the student photographs lining her blackboard to the student visitors who casually dropped by just for the chance to sweep her floor, and perhaps chat a bit. Alison spent many free afternoons watching her school's sporting events, where she expressed her interest in students outside of the classroom and also had the chance to informally speak with parents and family members about student academic success.

Managing Change

After three years of teaching in the same dilapidated building, the district office decided to sell her school building in order to raise funds and relocated Alison's school to a newer facility a few miles away. Despite the upheaval, Alison remained upbeat, seeing each incremental change as a positive step forward in the reform process. She commented, "I think it's going to be good. I think everything's going to get better." Alison was instrumental in the transition process, helping to pack and unpack boxes, set up science labs, and arrange for box lunches when the cafeteria was not ready on the first day of school. Over the next several years, Alison also moved into a mentor teacher role, teaching a reduced load and supporting newer teachers with planning, instruction, and classroom management. Because of the high teacher turnover at her school, Alison often had to begin again each fall with a completely new science department.

During her seven years in the schools, Alison devoted herself to her work both within and outside of the classroom. However, she also considered her future plans. At first, Alison expected to stay in urban teaching only for five years, until the district repaid her student loans, saying, "When I moved here, I said I'm going to do this for five years and just stick it through for five years." Then, as time passed, she felt committed to her students and planned to stay on until they graduated from high school. However, eventually she realized that there would always be another class coming through the pipeline, and she couldn't be there for all of them. Alison commented, "I realized that no matter what year I leave, I'm going to always feel like I'm abandoning the kids. And I don't want to, but there is no way that I'm not going to have new years of kids that I'm abandoning. So I can't use that as a reason anymore."

Moreover, Alison knew that she needed to complete a master's degree in order to qualify for a pay raise. She initially considered the field of science education, but on the recommendation of her principal ultimately settled on an urban administrator program that could be completed mostly online and included both a master's degree and an administrative certificate. Weighing her professional options, Alison knew that she did not want to teach forever, instead envisioning herself as a teacher mentor, school administrator, or urban education consultant.

Finding a New Role

After seven years of teaching and six years of working closely with the same principal, Alison's relationship with Dr. Jenkins began to deteriorate. Alison explained, "That year I had kind of fallen off really being in her tight inner circle." One of the first signs came when Alison applied for a professional development workshop in Costa Rica and Dr. Jenkins delayed writing her recommendation letter again and again, until Alison had to essentially do it herself if she wanted a complete application. Next, Alison started to notice that Dr. Jenkins did not always treat her staff fairly, at times favoring certain faculty over others.

For instance, Alison noted that Dr. Jenkins was quite lax about absences with one longtime English teacher, noting, "She let her kind of do whatever she wanted even though she was not very good at her job and just was never there." On the other hand, Alison felt that Dr. Jenkins was excessively hard on another colleague, a military veteran with an honorable discharge for disability who also missed a lot of school. Alison explained, "She was always given a lot of grief. Like, 'Why are you not coming in? We're not going to pay you.'" Alison felt that "there were lines," and certain teachers fit Dr. Jenkins's expectations while others did not.

On top of these interpersonal dynamics, her principal was also given greater control over the school's finances and decided to adjust their funding priorities for the coming year. Alison noted, "Normally I was in that conversation. That year I didn't know anything." Dr. Jenkins decided to fund a full-time parent liaison and promote the school's office staff while eliminating the mentor teacher positions. Alison was asked to return to full-time classroom teaching the following year, not in her field of chemistry but instead in biology. Alison explained that she did not mind the return to full-time teaching, but "I don't really like bio." It was at that point that she decided to consider other options.

Owning her home in William City and relatively settled there personally, Alison applied for several education-related positions both within and outside of the school district, including a graduation-support role at a neighboring high school, a position at the state education department, and a place on the district-level school support team. After an extensive interview process, Alison eventually landed an instructional support position as part of the district's school support network. In this role, she spent two years working with an interdisciplinary team of colleagues to improve instruction in fifteen high schools across the district. The work was challenging, though, with unprofessional colleagues and a lack of buy-in by the school-based personnel. Moreover, she often felt that just as she began to build trusting relationships with principals, she would get pulled out to deal with more pressing issues, and in that way "there was never any systematic change."

After several minor adjustments, including a move to a more well-run team and a redistribution of partner schools, Alison eventually decided that she would be better suited to a student support rather than an instructional support role, and applied within the network for this new position. Alison was quite pleased with her new responsibilities, which focused more directly on issues of attendance and school climate. For instance, before she felt that it was difficult to see the impact of her work. Alison noted, "Principals have a goal for student achievement, but in many cases it's so lofty. And principals have completely different definitions of what good instruction is." Moreover, she was frustrated that it often took over a year before she began to see any noticeable change in teachers' instruction, and only then if the principals supported her suggestions in their annual evaluations. However, in her new role she often saw the results of her efforts in a couple of weeks. Alison explained:

> For example, yesterday I was at a school looking at trends from November attendance data to now. And they're on the list of kids who had already missed fifteen days as of November. There were about twenty kids on that list. And then there were three or four who had like fifteen, nineteen absences in November, but then they have held steady with only one or two from November to [January]. Then today, I developed a template where the attendance monitor is going to track whether or not these kids are getting severely worse, holding steady, or getting better. And I'm going to be able to see in two weeks if it's making a difference.

Alison also liked how in this role she had more easily attainable targets, or what she termed "smaller wins." She went on, "This is such a small building that if we can get ten of these kids to just come two times more often, we can get to 94 percent, the AMO (annual measurable objective) target, which is huge." Finally, in her new role Alison liked being more integrated into a collaborative team and having the chance to interact with students on occasion.

In addition to her new professional responsibilities, Alison enjoyed greater flexibility in her work schedule: "If I need to make a dentist appointment, I can do that and come in at 9:30. If I want to take a week off in December, I can do that. You definitely have a level of freedom." In addition to her newfound flexibility, Alison also recognized that she was in a position of leadership that would take far longer to achieve in another, perhaps more stable, school district. Alison noted, "I don't know if I had been anywhere else that I would be in the kind of position I'm in with nine years in the system. Which is why it's kind of hard to leave the district." Her current level of seniority, along with its corresponding salary, made it difficult to consider any professional alternatives.

Returning to Schools

Although Alison remained fairly committed to staying within the William City school district long-term, she did eventually want to return to working in schools. She was attracted to the role of assistant principal and ultimately principal, but worried about the long hours required and the challenge of serving as the school's chief disciplinarian. She explained that as an assistant principal, "You're stuck there all hours of the night. You only have negative interactions with people and with kids. You can't miss any days, because the building falls apart when you're not there." However, despite her reservations Alison did see her current position as preparing her to ultimately move into school administration. She explained, "I enjoy the work and now it's going to actually be on my résumé that I have some experience in the disciplinary role. Which is nice because it's something that is a little bit of a void in my résumé. I've done some assistant principal–like things, but that whole disciplinary stuff was not really part of it."

Alison resolved that she would accept an assistant principal position when she found school leadership she could believe in: "I decided that I know that I do want to go back to the school, but in order to make those tradeoffs, I need to be doing something that I really want to do. So I need to make sure that I'm in a building where I really like the leadership, I really believe in the progression and where they're heading, so that I actually want to make that kind of commitment." Although Alison did not know when she would feel ready to make that transition, the path ahead to her next stage as an urban educational leader seemed quite clear.

MITCH

Although he has spent many years outside of the South, it is still possible to detect a slight Southern drawl in Mitch's speech. Born in North Carolina and raised in Maine, Virginia, Georgia, Mississippi, Alabama, and Nebraska, he grew up in a tight-knit military family, where his father advanced from enlisted radar technician to director of computer networks while his mother raised the children. Moving every few years, Mitch attended a variety of schools, from a predominantly low-income elementary school where he was one of a handful of White children to an arts magnet middle school to a highly academic high school, where he graduated as class valedictorian. Poised to enter the Air Force, Mitch's plans were derailed by back surgery; he ended up attending a local commuter university on a full scholarship while living at home, a decision he regretted because of the lack of student life on campus.

Committing to Education

Growing up, Mitch always felt a strong connection with his teachers and for many years dreamed of becoming a teacher himself. Mitch explained, "From kindergarten through junior high, my dream job was to be an elementary school teacher. We had to do a report on jobs when we were in eighth grade and I did it on elementary school teachers because that's what I wanted to be." He also held deep respect for his high school teachers, commenting on his chemistry teacher in particular: "I think that's why I'm a chemistry teacher, is because of him. It's just the way he explained things, and he expected so much out of us, and we learned so much." Mitch's connection with his former teachers continues to this day, through annual Christmas cards, graduation announcements, and even a trip back across the country in honor of his former choir director's retirement.

Although Mitch always felt drawn to education, his parents wanted their academically talented son to enter a more prestigious and lucrative field. He explained, "My family and others kept saying, 'You're going to waste yourself if you're a teacher.' It's like I'd be going down if I was a teacher. And they said, 'Why don't you be a doctor?' Always, 'Why don't you be a doctor?' Nobody ever said anything different, except doctor." Because of this pressure to go into medicine, Mitch entered college on the premedical track and earned dual degrees in both biology and chemistry, but he noted, "I just kept chugging along, but I wasn't really into it." Toward the end of college, when Mitch was faced with choosing his next steps, he began to shy away from medicine, noting, "I just felt like I can't do it. Because for me, my dream is to have a family, and I don't want something where I'm sitting down having dinner with my family and I get called and so you have to go and help this patient, which, I mean, that's what I'd have to do, but I don't want a job that makes me sacrifice my family."

Based on his concerns about work-family balance and his lack of interest in the field, Mitch decided to forgo medical school, still holding on to his interest in education: "I always still wanted to be a teacher, and I got in huge fights with my parents because I'm like, 'I'm just gonna go get an education degree.'" However, after researching graduate school in education, Mitch discovered that there were far more financial incentives to further his training in the sciences, noting, "If you go to grad school in chemistry, you're gonna get paid to go to school, and you will get the degree out of it. So I went to grad school in chemistry because I knew they would pay me, and it was a direct doctorate program." Mitch enrolled in graduate school in South Carolina in order to be closer to his grandparents and selected a program with a strong education focus, where he worked with several national leaders in chemical education. During graduate school, Mitch also chose an advisor who allowed him the flexibility to work as a teaching assistant for all five years because "he knew I loved to teach."

Against his parents' wishes, at the conclusion of graduate school Mitch decided to apply to Teach for America and was accepted into their William City corps, his third choice location. He explained that he chose Teach for America because it allowed him to "give back" while also trying out the field of teaching he had dreamed about for so long. Mitch explained, "My parents were really against me going into Teach for America, and I just said, 'I'm doing it. I have to do this because it's something that I need to know.'" Although Teach for America corps members are typically placed in the most challenging school contexts, Mitch ended up meeting a human resources official at the district office who directed him to an all-girls citywide magnet school with high academic standards. He accepted a position there teaching high school biology and chemistry and stayed for two years.

Finding His Place in Schools

At this school, Mitch developed positive relationships with the vast majority of his students and challenged them to reach high academic standards in his classes, even pitting class periods against each other in a race for the highest test scores. He explained that he saw it as his role as a teacher to "push them to do more," bringing K-12 science education up to the level required at top colleges and universities. He devoted a considerable amount of time and money to his classroom, spending several hundreds of dollars each month on supplies so that his students could have engaging and hands-on learning opportunities in the sciences, noting, "My top priority is finding a good lesson to teach my students that will reach them and make them excited about the material." Mitch also became involved with students in numerous ways outside of the classroom, advising the sophomore class, coaching an academic trivia team, and planning a school-wide family picnic. His efforts were rewarded with the nomination for a national teaching award at the end of his second year.

Although he had positive relationships with students, Mitch often felt out of place with his fellow teachers, many of whom were long established at his magnet school and shied away from departmental collaboration. Mitch tried to strengthen the faculty community by initiating a popular series of Friday happy hours, attended by about eight to ten sociable teachers from across the building. While feeling too young for his school's community, at twenty-seven Mitch also felt too old for the Teach for America community. Although he appreciated the pedagogical support he received in content area group meetings, he rarely spent time with his Teach for America colleagues in social settings. On top of it all, Mitch was living in a city for the first time in his life and felt isolated and alone, far away from his family. "I feel very lonely in William City," he admitted.

Little by little, Mitch also began to lose confidence in the educational system he so respected. Mitch came into teaching with the belief that his students could be successful in science. He noted, "Our children can do it. Our children are capable. They just need to be taught and need to be pushed. Looking at some of my best students, I think that our country can really go places, that our future is bright." However, over time he became discouraged by what he perceived to be a fundamental lack of collaboration between schools and families. He explained, "In William City, everything is the teacher's fault. And I don't believe either way it's 100 percent anybody's fault, and I don't know if it's exactly 50-50, but the teacher cannot pour information into a student's head." Mitch's disillusionment only grew after he received an improvement plan from his school's administration, which was not coupled with the promised support. Mitch explained:

> The [improvement plan] is a contract that they have to do something to help you, which she said, in my case, she was going to give me time off to go observe teachers; never happened. Send me to classroom management workshops; never happened. Gather materials for me on classroom management; never happened. Come and observe my class several times; half the time she came half the class period, that's all. They never gave me the support.

After that point, Mitch explained that he no longer trusted his school's leadership to support his efforts, noting, "Since then, I've never felt comfortable with the administration."

Exploring School Reform

At the end of his second year in the classroom and the conclusion of his Teach for America commitment, Mitch decided he was ready to leave his school and explore his professional options. Looking within the field of education, Mitch considered a central role in the Teach for America organization, but ultimately decided upon another classroom position as part of the Knowledge Is Power Program (KIPP) school network. He explained what attracted him to this new school context: "Just the sense of community. I love everybody that works there. Everybody is in that same mentality."

Also, as the school building was currently under construction, Mitch was excited about the opportunity to design and stock his own classroom chemistry laboratory, noting, "[The principal] said any questions about the construction or what needs to go in my classroom go through me. I get to make all the decisions. And she told me, anything I need to let her know and she'll order it." Moreover, this KIPP school was located in a rural area of the South, only an hour away from his parents and even closer to his grandparents, "so that's very appealing," he noted. "At least I'd have somebody around. Living there, I'd at least have somebody all the time I could do something with, whereas in William City I don't."

Initially, Mitch was energized by the work of starting up a new school. He felt far more connected with the other staff, commenting, "I feel like we're one, on the same page. I feel like part of a family." He appreciated that the school held common expectations for student behavior and commented on the students' "awesome sense of wanting to learn." Despite challenges, such as scouring local churches for chairs on the night before school started, he noted, "I've never felt more fulfilled." During this time, he became close with his school principal, who impressed him with her level of dedication to the school and students. He noted that she mopped the floors, learned alongside the students, and was an integral part of the school team. He also appreciated finally being treated as a professional, explaining, "that's the most important thing, being treated like a professional, and giving me my professional respect." At this new school, Mitch once again took on a number of out-of-classroom responsibilities, including tutoring below-grade-level students in math and mentoring current Teach for America corps members.

As the school year progressed, however, Mitch began to wear down from exhaustion. Regularly staying at the school from 7:15 a.m. until 8:00 p.m., Mitch recognized that he was in an unsustainable situation but resolved that things would improve once the school better established its routines and expectations. He was frustrated, however, that not all staff members put in equal effort. In one instance, Mitch found himself supervising eighty students in a study hall without support from his colleagues, noting, "We say things and we're all supposed to help each other, and some people don't necessarily do that." He was beginning to recognize some problems in his school culture, noting, "A lot of the things we do at KIPP feel very magical—I really thought it was magical when I applied. But when you're in it, it's not as magical because there are a lot of little problems." He maintained that he was still happier than in William City, feeling more connected to the local community and explaining, "Now my stress comes from being extremely exhausted, as opposed to feeling like I'm being hammered. [In William City] I felt like I was always under attack by the administration."

Drained Out of Teaching

During his second year with KIPP, Mitch's situation became intolerable, and midway through the year he made the decision that this would be his last, despite an informal three-year commitment. First, he once again felt that his dedication to the school was not shared by all, explaining, "I got frustrated because of the mantra of the school when we first started: 'If somebody needs help, you help them out.' We do everything for the students, so I always sacrifice myself. But not everybody was like that."

Second, because of a last-minute scheduling change, Mitch's teaching load expanded to include six block periods. He explained:

> So I taught periods one through six. I taught from 8:00 until 4:00, with 15 minutes for lunch. And then I had a planning period from 4:00 to 5:00. But the students knew that and so they came in for help. And then I'd have students from about 5:00 to 7:00 for extra help, or meetings. And then I'd have to drive the kids home. And then I'd go home and plan and crash, and then come back and do it the next day. I just got so burned out.

Mitch recognized that much of this workload was his own doing, as he volunteered for numerous responsibilities outside of the classroom, such as course scheduling. He noted, "If I would have been just focused on my classroom, things would have been different. But I tried to do everything." His workload was so immense that when he ultimately left, the principal replaced him with three people.

The third, crucial factor in Mitch's departure was the deterioration of his relationship with the school principal. He noted, "The principal essentially had what we called the inner circle and the outer circle. And so there were certain teachers in the inner circle and the rest of you were on the outside. So anything the teachers on the inner circle did was okay. But those on the outer circle, not necessarily." He faced a number of situations where he felt unsupported by his principal. In particular, he felt that she often sided with students when dealing with matters of disruptive behavior, which were becoming more and more common with the arrival of a difficult freshman class.

After four years of teaching, Mitch decided that it was time to move on. In particular, he noted, "I thought I would enjoy teaching more than I do. I love it, but I didn't think it would be as discipline-heavy, and that part I don't enjoy." However, he struggled with the decision, particularly because he wanted to feel like a success. Mitch explained, "I didn't want to be a failure at teaching, which I thought I was. I wanted to be a much better teacher, and I didn't think I was going to have that where I was." Mitch was also still under a lot of pressure from his parents to consider alternatives to K-12 teaching, his father encouraging him to move from the high school to a community college, and his mother still wanting him to make a lot of money, something he recognized as close to impossible in education.

He finally confronted his parents about their pressure, noting, "My dad mentions it all the time, and I get frustrated. This time I explained why I feel the way I do. I told him it bothers me. He doesn't understand; he thinks I'm doing the lowest thing I can. He doesn't know why I worked so hard and spent nine years in college. I just wish they could be happy for what I am doing." Mitch considered a future as a school administrator, a district superintendent, or a leader within the KIPP or Teach for America movements. He even played with his longtime dream of elementary school teaching. But he recognized that immediately, he just needed a new job.

Mitch described his decision to leave teaching without another position lined up as "probably the scariest thing I've ever done in my life," having gone from college to graduate school to Teach for America without so much as a two-week break. However, on a tip from his former graduate mentor, Mitch connected with a national nonprofit organization in the field of chemistry and secured a position in their education division, moving once again to a large city for this job. He was in this role for three and a half years, working on their high school textbook design, offering professional development for chemistry teachers, and managing high school chemistry clubs. Although he at times got frustrated with the low pay and the incompetence of his supervisors, he genuinely enjoyed his work with chemistry teachers around the country:

> I like the interactions with people; I love the interactions with teachers. So all the teachers I've worked with, I've learned so much about education. I interact with so many different teachers and we have high school teachers that run our workshops, and nine of them I've become really good friends with and they teach all over the country. It's so amazing for me to see that.

While he continued to work very long hours, Mitch did find the time to go to the gym, where he focused on losing weight and increasing his fitness.

Considering His Impact

Although generally content in his current position, and soon to be promoted, Mitch still dreamed of returning to more direct work with schools and students, noting that he would like to "have some type of effect on kids. That's always been my passion. I definitely want to have an impact on kids at some level." While working full-time, Mitch also volunteered as a reading buddy at a local elementary school, where he worked with the same young boy for three years and observed a positive impact on his performance in class. He was also planning an eventual return to graduate school in either educational leadership or business administration, to prepare for a more administrative position with the schools. While he was not entirely clear on what direction this would take him, he envisioned a number of possibilities, including opening a math and science–focused charter school network, serving as a science curriculum coordinator for a school district, or working on school budgeting.

Mitch also wanted to move out of the city and into what he considered a real community, commenting, "I'm starting to think that I want to settle down, be a part of the community. Get married, have kids. I want a family. But the community piece is very important to me, and I don't feel a part of a community right now." He still admired his own former teachers, who "taught generations—they would teach parents of kids," as well as many of the teachers he currently works with, who stay in the classroom well into their seventies. He also wanted to make sure that in the future he worked more directly with students, noting, "I want to be a teacher and a leader at the same time. I definitely miss the interaction with students. That's one of the pieces that I miss." He hoped, in time, to become an integral part of a school, community, and the lives of children.

THEMES

Alison and Mitch represent two individuals within a large and growing group of teachers: those who leave classroom teaching but remain within the education sector. Ingersoll and May's (2010) recent national analysis demonstrates that this group of teachers includes almost 20 percent of all departures, whereas those who leave education altogether comprise only about 9 percent of departures. In recent years, these shifting career pathways have been held up as a legitimate form of attrition (Quartz et al., 2008), particularly in the field of urban education where they supply much-needed educational leaders (Olsen & Anderson, 2007). Moreover, these differentiated educational roles appear to offer teachers the opportunities for the ongoing growth and widening influence they need to remain satisfied as professionals (Margolis, 2008), perhaps serving as a means to retaining talented educators in the field, if not in the classroom.

Theme #1: Shifters Faced Challenges Related to Workload and Relationships

Alison's and Mitch's journeys have some important parallels that help illuminate what teachers experience when they shift out of classroom teaching into education-related positions. First, both Alison and Mitch came into teaching with a long-standing dedication to the field of education. Both considered becoming teachers when they were young, and although they took temporary detours, Alison to her chemistry major and Mitch through graduate school, both returned to the idea of teaching again and again until they finally reached the classroom. Because of his parents' resistance to the idea, Mitch even had to take a stand in order to pursue what he considered his dream. Alison's and Mitch's experiences reinforce, in a new way, the importance of teachers' intentions in constructing their career pathways, offering a form of professional resilience in the face of challenging workplace contexts.

Next, both Alison's and Mitch's years in the classroom were character- ized by close relationships with both students and colleagues. Alison made it her top priority to provide emotional support to students facing difficult life circumstances. Mitch focused more on academic support, but likewise developed strong emotional bonds with his students, distribut- ing individualized notes and gifts to students during holidays and at the end of each year. While both have currently moved on to nonclassroom roles with far less student interaction, they openly voice how much they miss students and hope to return to more student-centered work at some point in the future. In addition to connecting with their students, Alison and Mitch also constructed positive relationships with colleagues. Alison was voted "best team player" among the staff at her school and Mitch fostered interaction first through happy hours and later by seeking out a familial workplace climate. Day and Gu (2010) note that effective educa- tors develop strong, positive relationships with their students, while Johnson, Kraft, and Papay (2012) stress the importance of colleagues in shaping professional satisfaction. Alison and Mitch seem to echo the idea that those with long-lasting impact in the field of education put relation- ships at the center of their practice.

Despite their solid commitment to the field and positive collegial interactions, both Alison and Mitch came up against difficult workplace conditions. Mitch cited exhaustion and burnout as his primary reasons for leaving teaching, whereas Alison was disappointed by the loss of funding for her mentor teacher position. However, both of these concerns stemmed, to a certain extent, from what they independently termed "in- ner circle" politics. Both Alison and Mitch, previously close with their principals, felt they had somehow been placed on the outside of impor- tant decision making and subject to objectionable estimations of their work.

Moreover, they seem to have lost trust in their formerly valued lead- ers. Ladd (2011) highlights the central role of the school principal in influ- encing teachers' retention and attrition decisions, and Bryk and Schnei- der (2003) stress the importance of trust in particular. The experiences of Alison and Mitch certainly reinforce the notion that interactions with school leadership, particularly those that involve dynamics of inclusion and exclusion from power (Skaalvik & Skaalvik, 2011), are pivotal in shaping career trajectories.

Theme #2: Shifters Remaining Broadly Committed to the Field of Education

What makes the experiences of these shifters unique is that, faced with difficult workplace conditions, these teachers chose not to transition to another school or leave teaching altogether, but instead to shift into edu- cation-related roles. After deciding to leave their current positions, both Alison and Mitch looked solely for work within the education sector, considering a variety of roles but not once contemplating leaving the field altogether. This education-focused lens stands in stark contrast to the experiences of the stayers who sought out improved school contexts as well as the leavers who departed what they considered their temporary jobs for their real career paths. Instead, Alison and Mitch both remained committed to education as a whole, seeking only the best place for themselves within the larger field.

Their career decisions lie at the heart of the interaction between biography and workplace context. While previous research has demonstrated how challenging working conditions can effectively push teachers out of schools (Borman & Dowling, 2008; Johnson et al., 2012), workplace context alone cannot determine where they go next. With Alison and Mitch it is clear that initial motivations and commitment to the field shaped their next professional steps exclusively within the field of education. Biography also plays a role here. Traditional notions of gender, in combination with social pressure from family and friends, may have influenced Mitch to consider more high-status options such as educational leadership over and above alternatives like elementary teaching. Likewise, Alison's appreciation of her newfound flexibility may delay her return to a school-based position. Together, Alison and Mitch show how important it is to not only understand the factors that shape why teachers stay and leave, but also the factors that influence where they go next. In these cases, inner circle politics and workplace conditions may have expedited their departure from the classroom, but life experiences and professional commitments shaped their next professional steps.

Theme #3: Shifters Drew upon Professionalism and Agency to Shape Their Careers

Grounded in lenses shaped by past goals and commitments, Alison's and Mitch's career trajectories were also influenced by their areas of professional expertise. At the time of their departure from the classroom, both Alison and Mitch had completed graduate degrees with training beyond classroom teaching. Alison earned a master's degree in urban education with an administrator's certificate, while Mitch held a doctorate in chemistry. These degrees appear to have opened doors for them professionally that may not have been available had they only held teaching certificates.

For instance, Alison's move to the central office seems to have been facilitated by her academic background as well as her classroom experiences, while Mitch's national role in chemistry curriculum development could only be possible with his advanced context expertise. In these ways, both Alison and Mitch appear to have been set up for success in their career transitions to educational leaders, easily securing and succeeding in education-related roles. Likewise, Mitch recognizes that if he is to shift again into school or district leadership, he will need to continue developing his expertise by returning to school yet again. In this way, their experiences support Meier's (2012) notion that teaching-specific degrees have low exchange value in other fields, including within other areas of education.

Finally, although Alison and Mitch have recently transitioned into new positions, their careers remain dynamic as they explore the best way to make their contribution. Since leaving teaching, Alison has moved twice within the district office and plans to shift into school administration when the conditions are right. Likewise, Mitch is considering an offer of promotion within his current organization but down the road would like to move into school or district leadership. Their continually evolving pathways reflect the dynamic careers of today's teachers as well as an ongoing search for efficacy within the workplace that appears to define career movements. Mitch would like to be in a position where he can have a more direct impact upon children, whereas Alison is drawn to attainable targets and measurable goals so that she can see the results of her efforts. Together, these goals and their attempts to attain them point to the enduring role of efficacy in defining not only classroom work but broader efforts within the field of education.

Together, Alison and Mitch paint a picture not of overwhelmed novices who left teaching discouraged and disillusioned, but instead of professional educators who are resilient in the face of challenges and use their own agency to define for themselves what constitutes a meaningful career in education. Although displeased with particular aspects of their workplace contexts, both Alison and Mitch used their opportunities for career transitions not to run away from teaching, but instead to build upon their advanced expertise and transition into leadership positions. They continue to seek out contexts that are better suited to reaching their goals and where they feel a greater sense of efficacy in their work. And they remain committed both to educating young people and to sustaining relationships at the center of their professional lives. Alison's and Mitch's experiences highlight professional resilience (Day & Gu, 2010; Yonezawa, Jones, & Singer, 2011) not as a means of enduring negative situations, but rather as a way to reshape their own work lives for the better. And they showcase the tremendous potential of teacher agency in continually pursuing the conditions that will allow them to best impact schools and students.

FIVE

Those Who Left

It's challenging and interesting and I feel like it has a purpose.
—Charlotte, of her new job in government defense

The third group of case study teachers were either in the process of transitioning out of the field of education altogether or had already entered a new career. Alexandra earned a second master's degree in public health and was looking to secure a position in that field; Charlotte, after a transitional period in information technology, was delighted with her new job in government defense; and Tara earned a second bachelor's degree in forensic science and was currently working as a forensic analyst.

This group of case study teachers was unique in that they all entered teaching in an exploratory manner, with the possibility of turning teaching into a long-term career. However, after a short period in the classroom all came to the conclusion that, for them, education was only a temporary occupation rather than an enduring profession. Their narratives illustrate the critically important nature of the first few years in the classroom for helping novice educators settle on a career path, the difficult process of transitioning out of the classroom, and the enduring nature of teaching both within and outside of the classroom walls.

ALEXANDRA

Alexandra grew up outside of New York City, where she attended a science and technology magnet high school. Alexandra explained that she had always been interested in the connections between science and people, hoping to find herself in a role where she could translate between the two. At a liberal arts college, she double majored in biology and

theatre while considering careers in medicine, technical roles in the theatre, and psychology research. It was not until her senior year of college
that Alexandra began to consider teaching. Knowing from her experiences as a tutor and a leader that she excelled at teaching, Alexandra
applied and was accepted to Teach for America. She hoped that teaching
would allow her to make an impact while spending two years figuring
out what she wanted to do with her life.

Getting Involved

Through Teach for America, Alexandra was placed in a biology classroom in a large comprehensive high school, where she received some
support from her department chair but felt anonymous in the school as a
whole. Although she struggled with maintaining student engagement in
the classroom, she made positive connections with students outside of
class through the school's theatre program. She originally only volunteered to assist, but ultimately ended up directing a school-wide produc-
tion of *The Wiz*. Moreover, while she participated in Teach for America's
support network, pursuing her master's in teaching as required by the
state and attending professional development sessions, she at times felt
disconnected from the rest of her cohort, which she described as a "popu-
larity contest."

Although she felt a sense of accomplishment during her first year in
the classroom, toward the end of her second year in the classroom and
the conclusion of her Teach for America commitment Alexandra began to
feel overwhelmed and disillusioned with the profession. She was particularly frustrated by the lack of commitment from the students and parents.
With half of her colleagues leaving the school, Alexandra decided to look
for a position in a more supportive school environment. She explained
that she would like a school that was "supportive of its teachers to the
point where, 'Oh, that's something that you need? Let's see if maybe we
can get it.' Or where the administration actually knows or respects that
we are putting in a lot of work. Those people who are deserving get some
kind of recognition."

After looking around for more supportive school contexts in William
City, Alexandra accepted a position at a reform-oriented school called
Brilliance Charter School, first as a technology teacher and later as the
technology coordinator. She chose this school because she liked the principal's leadership and because she would work a reduced teaching load.
She also noted that she was not sure where else to turn: "My biggest
issue, the reason I don't just say I'm going to drop it at the end of the year
and just move on is because I don't know what I want to do. I'm running
into the typical twentysomething, what am I going to do with myself?"
Although Alexandra saw all jobs as inherently temporary, saying, "I
didn't go into teaching thinking I was going to be there long-term," she

resolved to stay in education a few more years in the new charter school context.

Finding Her Place in Schools

Alexandra ended up staying five years at Brilliance Charter School in a quasiadministrative role as the internship and technology coordinator. In this position, Alexandra was responsible for a wide variety of tasks, including developing, teaching, and securing placements for the school's internship program, raising money to build a new computer lab, ordering school supplies, running professional development workshops, modeling the use of SMART Boards, supporting teachers' data analysis, maintaining the school's website, hiring new teachers, and enrolling new students. In this role, Alexandra had rewards as well as frustrations, explaining, "There were moments when I absolutely loved it, and there were other moments when I'm like, 'what the hell am I doing?'"

Professionally, she was pleased that she, along with two colleagues, had become vital to the school's functioning. She explained, "There were certain people at the school that were really at the center of the building, so people would come to you with a question whether or not you knew the answer. It sort of started cycling around us, and we were also there [a] long [time]." Alexandra enjoyed being central to the school's functioning and did not mind taking on extra responsibilities that needed to get done.

At the same time, however, she was frustrated that students did not always follow through on their responsibilities. She explained that some of her greatest frustrations came when she worked hard to find internship placements for students and then they did not show up or were rude to their supervisors. She lamented, "If I matched exactly what you wanted, exactly in the location you wanted, exactly doing what you said you wanted and then you don't show up or you show up like an hour late every day, it started to grate on me." Alexandra felt that her efforts were not shared equally with her student partners.

Finding Her Passion

Despite the ups and downs of her five years at Brilliance Charter School, Alexandra had already decided that, education being a temporary occupation, her real passion lay in the field of public health. She particularly envisioned herself working at the local or state level in disaster preparedness, imagining this to be another way of connecting science with people. During her time at Brilliance, Alexandra pursued a second master's degree in public health through a blended learning program at a prestigious local university. At first she was not admitted to the program because the admissions requirements included direct medical experience, but ultimately Alexandra convinced the program that her work as an emergency medical technician during college, her volunteer experiences, and her years as a science teacher constituted the type of prior experience they wanted. Although ultimately admitted, she was one of only a few students in the program without clinical expertise as a doctor or nurse.

Transitioning Out of the Classroom

After five years at Brilliance Charter School, after earning her master's of public health degree, Alexandra decided it was time to formally leave the field of education. Her choice followed the departure of her principal, a man whom she held in high regard and whom she called a "pillar" of the school. In his place was a newly trained principal who started doing things in her own way. Alexandra explained:

> My issue was that she kept bringing on her people. The person that took over the career coordinator had been a friend of hers; she put him in charge of a career program, which he knew nothing about. She then hired another friend of hers who is a lawyer, never worked in the schools, to be one of our administrators. It was starting to become not an environment that those of us who had been there a while felt comfortable with.

In addition to the change in administration was Alexandra's exhaustion from eight years of hard work in schools. Alexandra commented, "I was too stressed at the job. I took it too seriously. I let it affect me too much." These three factors, her preparation for the field of public health, a change in the school's administration, and her physical and mental exhaustion, together indicated that the time had come to resign. Despite colleagues begging her to return, Alexandra was resolved to leave education and make a career change into public health.

After an extended vacation with her parents to see the national parks, Alexandra focused her attention on the task of applying for new jobs in the field of public health. Despite her advanced degree in the field, Alexandra was unable to land a position. She applied for a wide range of jobs, from health education to epidemiology research to managerial and assistantship positions, but could not break into the field. Repeatedly, she was told that she needed more office experience, and Alexandra also sensed that she needed a stronger professional network in the field. After several months of trying to secure a position, when she was beginning to run out of money, Alexandra settled for an administrative assistant position in the school district's central office. Alexandra explained, "What I'm trying to do is build the office [skills] in the day, and the other thing is I'm building the networking at night." In the evening, Alexandra volunteered for local public health groups like the Red Cross, citizen CPR training, and AIDS prevention programs.

Alexandra noted that not only was she gaining necessary office skills, but her new job also offered her some recuperation from the stress of working as a teacher and administrator. She described every day at Brilliance as "crisis mode." Alexandra said, "The kids go crazy and they do their own thing, and there's a fight or someone leaves and like then someone has to stay and cover or something has to get done because it has to get done by tomorrow, and we didn't do it last week. I just felt like every day was like that." However, with more flexibility each day, she began focusing on her health. She joined a gym, was losing weight, and training to run a 5K. She stopped taking antidepressants and felt " mentally some of the healthiest I've been." And she was participating in a singles club to make friends and seek a romantic partner. This new phase in her professional life afforded her the freedom to construct a more favorable work-life balance.

Preparing to Move, Again

Looking forward, Alexandra planned to stay at the district office only long enough to gain the experience she needed, saying, "I applied to this job with the hope that, if I did like a year, year and a half at this job, I would have more of the 'experience' that some of those coordinator-type positions [need]." Then her plan was to leverage her office skills and professional network to secure a position in public health in William City. Long-term, she envisioned herself moving from a local to a more national level, such as working at the Centers for Disease Control in Atlanta. Throughout this transition, Alexandra noted the important connection between the field of education and the field of public health, saying she was moving "from academic learning for young children to lifestyle learning for all people." She explained, "I'm out of the classroom, but I still feel like I'm teaching. I'm teaching the people I'm working with." Although she was officially transitioning out of teaching, she brought her instructional skills along with her to inform her work. Alexandra had not yet completed her transition from the field of education, but she dedicated herself to securing the training, experience, and professional network necessary to move into public health.

CHARLOTTE

Charlotte came from a long line of scientists and engineers and from the time she was a child envisioned herself becoming a scientist. "I was just a born scientist type," she explained, "From day one, I was always really into math and really into science. Even my hobbies were all kind of science. I was very into exploring things." She grew up in Alabama and South Carolina with what she called a "liberal, feminist, nonreligious" mother and attended space camp four years in a row, which sparked a lifelong interest in space science. For high school, Charlotte enrolled in a public boarding school focused on math and science education, a college preparatory program where she built strong relationships with some of her teachers. Later, she became one of the only women majoring in physics at a prestigious technical university, where she found that she enjoyed teaching while working as a calculus teaching assistant.

Charlotte always saw herself as an academic, explaining, "My plan was always to finish my undergraduate degree, go get my master's and my PhD, and spend the rest of my life in academia, doing research and maybe occasionally, begrudgingly having to teach an undergrad." She did give pause, however, after seeing a Teach for America poster on campus one day during her senior year. Although she was intrigued by the possibility of teaching, she felt that she could not take a two-year break from her plans to attend graduate school. Charlotte said, "I was just not, at that point in my life, prepared to commit two years to something with being in grad school and everything breathing down my neck." Instead, Charlotte went directly into a doctoral program in astrophysics.

After three years in graduate school at a male-dominated institution, dealing with challenging relationships with some department faculty, Charlotte decided that she wanted to transfer to another institution to complete her degree. However, she needed to arrange a transitional period between programs. She explained her reasoning:

> I had to come up with something that was kind of a transitional thing. I started thinking what I could do, and I thought, you know, maybe I can work doing research-type things. But then I was like, well why don't I just do this thing that I had thought about doing before, but felt like I couldn't give the time to, and that was do something like a Teach for America–type program. That would be perfect. It's a set amount of time, and it won't necessarily make sense to anyone who knows me, but it's something that I want to do. I felt like it would be at least a productive use of my time.

Charlotte withdrew from her graduate program with a master's degree and decided to pursue the alternative certification program in William City because of a personal contact there.

Fostering Academic Success

Charlotte's first year of teaching took place at an alternative high school for students who had not been successful in traditional school programs, where she was in charge of earth science and physics. Although student attendance in her classes typically hovered around 30 percent, she did have a core group of about three students who showed up every day and took their academic work in physics quite seriously.

Charlotte was pleased with the progress and potential of these core students and supported them on their paths to college.

Although she got along well with most of her colleagues, Charlotte did at times become frustrated with the incompetence she observed at her school. She noted, "There's definitely teachers who just don't care, and they've figured out how to make it easy on themselves. They don't really try." Even more frustrating was her administration. Charlotte explained, "There is no bigger problem [than the administration]. And it's the main reason why I'm essentially looking for somewhere else to go next year. Because I actually cannot work with them, not just because they're incompetent, but because they're actually bad. Basically, our principal is a used car salesman." At the conclusion of the school year, Charlotte's school was shut down by the district due to low test scores, a decision she learned about from the local newspaper.

Starting Over

For the following school year, Charlotte secured a position at the most academically successful citywide magnet school, where she ended up working for three school years. She described her second year in the classroom like first-year teaching all over again because she had to re-learn classroom management and instructional and assessment skills for the new, high-achieving school context. Charlotte explained, "It was almost like the first year got erased" from her two-year teaching plan.

Then, the following year she was asked to step into the advanced placement (AP) physics course. Charlotte reflected, "I was pretty excited about that because it's taught as a second-year physics course and most of the students have taken [first-year physics] and now they're seniors and they're taking AP physics and they're also taking AP calc, so they were pretty high performance students." In retrospect, Charlotte considered that to be her greatest year in the classroom, saying, "That was probably my best year because I did feel like I knew what I was doing and I felt like I had made some important changes based on the lessons I'd learned." Although she had originally only planned to teach for two years, she decided to stay one more while also reapplying to graduate school.

At that point, things started to go downhill, as the school's new principal did not maintain the same stringent school culture. Once again, Charlotte explained:

> I felt like the climate at the school had taken a nosedive, and I'm not the only person who felt this way. Basically, we lost a lot of teachers and there were all these meetings, teachers were just freaking out. People who were in the three- to ten-year range were leaving because they're like, "I can get out." People who were in the "I've been here twenty-five years" were like "I don't know what to do. I can't really leave

because I can't retire yet and it's like, I will lose everything if I leave now basically." And so they were really depressed. It was kind of a nightmare.

Within that context, Charlotte decided in October that this would be her last year in the classroom, even though, with full-time teaching, she had not found the time to seriously pursue graduate school applications. She resolved to "keep my head above water" until the end of the year and then apply for jobs outside of the classroom.

Returning to Her Original Plans

Charlotte had only intended to teach for two years, and while her detour into the classroom ended up lasting a full four years, she saw herself as returning to her original trajectory. Charlotte said, at that point:

> I was done with teaching. I was like, "I'm ready to get on with my life." I guess I never thought I would have my mind changed to where I wanted to be a teacher. It was never my dream to be a teacher. And I guess I allowed for the possibility that I could love it so much that I could just want to do it forever, but that didn't happen. I didn't think it would happen. Anyway, it didn't. And so I was kind of like, "experiment over." Time to proceed with my life.

Her departure from the classroom also coincided with a decision point in her personal life. Her boyfriend of several years was dragging his feet about getting married and Charlotte felt that "I hit one of those points in life where you're going to have to evaluate where are you and where are you going and what are you doing and why is my life like this." The same summer that she left teaching, Charlotte also broke things off with her boyfriend and moved into her own house in William City.

Then Charlotte entered into what she called an "extended vacation" for the summer and fall. Asked to teach as an adjunct instructor in an earth-space science certificate program and also at a local community college, Charlotte figured she had enough income coming in from her part-time jobs to take some time to "decompress." She felt that this time of partial employment was fully warranted because "after my last year of teaching, I was a wreck. I was like, 'I need to get my life together. I'm just going to take this time. I have some me time.'" Charlotte spent this time tending to her physical and mental health. She described this time in her life: "It was great. I got like nine hours of sleep every night. I read a lot of books. This was the best thing I've ever done." She also enjoyed working with the teachers in the space science certificate program, whom she described as fun and creative, explaining, "I feel like I am still a little bit in the teaching world without actually having to deal with students that are under twenty." After about six months of recuperation, Charlotte decided it was time to start finding that job she really wanted.

Facing an Extended Transition

Still focused on returning to graduate school, Charlotte decided, "I'll apply for jobs at universities and then I can maybe take some classes for free and then segue into grad school." She ended up working for one year in the information technology (IT) department of a large university, managing a research database. She sarcastically described her responsibilities: "I did 'exciting things' like creating accounts for people and deleting accounts for people." Charlotte's inquisitive mind found this job to be extremely boring, and she was constantly "watching the minutes tick by so I can leave when it hits 5:00." Moreover, her boss refused to let her take courses at the university. "I was like, 'I'm kind of interested in taking some classes.' And my boss was like, 'Absolutely not.' If you wanted to take a daytime class, it says right in the handbook, as long as you work your full day you can. My boss was like, 'No. We need you here all the time.'" Frustrated and bored, Charlotte once again began seeking a job she could get excited about.

Finding Her Real Career

After an extensive application process, Charlotte finally landed a job that she loved, working in government defense. She explained, "Now I'm in this weird position that I have pretty much never been in where I wake up every day and I think, 'Wow. I love my job. I can't wait to go to work. This is so interesting.'" Charlotte planned to stay there for the next thirty years, saying, "I feel like I found it. My plan is to stay there until I die or retire." While there were some day-to-day frustrations, such as dealing with a large government bureaucracy and learning to adapt to military culture, generally she saw a bright future for herself in government defense.

Although this career path veered from her original plan of going into academia, she felt like it used her knowledge and skills:

> I think for a long time with teaching or the IT job, you know, I went to school for so long and I worked so hard to learn all these things that I am, frankly, not using at all. It was really depressing to be in that situation, like "Why did I kill myself for so long?" And now I feel like it's finally paying off. All of that work I did I can actually use. I really feel like I'm using all my skills.

Moreover, she felt like she was being held to high expectations at her current job and there was plenty of room to grow, noting, "You look around at the people you're working with and the people who've been there for twenty years, they're still having to learn new things every day. So that's part of it, it's like everyone is constantly having to learn and improve but I love that. That's what I like doing. I don't want to be making the same widget every day. That's not fun."

And finally, Charlotte felt that her new job had purpose: "I feel like it's important stuff. It's important that somebody does it and I'm doing it and that's awesome." Altogether, although Charlotte was not on the exact academic path she envisioned, she was delighted with her career trajectory out of education and into government defense.

TARA

Tall and soft-spoken, Tara grew up with a day-care teacher mother and a New York City police officer father and was raised in what she called "the good part of the Bronx." She maintains a relationship with one of her elementary school teachers to this day and attended a racially mixed intermediate school focused on unity. In the seventh grade, Tara learned about the field of neonatology from her science textbook and decided that she wanted to become a neonatal nurse.

However, her father pushed her even farther, inspiring a lifelong dream of becoming a doctor. Mentored by her college-educated aunt and her father, Tara enrolled in a biomedical research program within a large comprehensive high school which took an hour and a half to reach each day by public transportation. Although her sister feared that she would get "beat up" at this school, Tara thrived in what she characterized as a supportive "microcosm" within the larger building. The program's determined director saw Tara's potential and guided her toward prestigious college preparatory summer institutes and ultimately toward a northeastern liberal arts college education.

In college, Tara pursued a biology major but also had the freedom to concentrate in West African studies, where she studied West African art, dance, and film. Although she remained committed to attending medical school, Tara was frustrated by the challenges of organic chemistry and felt that she needed a backup plan within the sciences. She decided to apply to the combined bachelor's and master's program in biology in order to learn laboratory research skills and ended up working for several years in the lab of a successful female professor who served as a positive role model for women in the sciences.

At the conclusion of her master's degree, Tara was in the process of preparing for the Medical College Admissions Test (MCAT) when personal matters intervened and she felt that she had to make a choice between family and career. She explained, "I think at the time, things were cut and dried to me. I was like, family's first because time here is too short. And for me to just focus on med school, I didn't want to do that at the time. But now that I think on it, I wonder if I could have juggled both." Given her choice at the time, Tara put family first, deferred her application to medical school, and put her lab skills to use in the field of pharmaceutical research and development, where she enjoyed greater flexibility and fewer time demands than a medical career.

Switching Careers

Tara ended up working in the field of pharmaceuticals for almost ten years at two different companies. However, as she reached thirty years of age she began to reassess her professional direction. Her company was attempting to globalize and evolving from a family-friendly culture to a high-productivity culture. With this growth, Tara was also asked to spend more and more time out of the lab and behind a computer screen writing up lab protocols. At this same juncture, Tara wanted to grow her family and find a career where she could use her lab skills while also maintaining work-life balance.

After considering varying options from a return to medicine to dress-making, Tara was convinced by her educator husband to try teaching and decided to relocate closer to her husband's job to cut down on his commute. From a personal connection Tara learned about William City Pride, a small and reform-oriented academy which she perceived as a supportive microcosm within the larger district, similar to her own high school experience. She accepted a job teaching science there and moved with her husband and two children to William City.

Struggling to Learn the Craft of Teaching

A first-year teacher who postponed formal teacher education, Tara struggled with the responsibilities of daily planning and preparation. Assigned out-of-field to a chemistry class, although her expertise lay in biology, Tara also did not know how to begin teaching this challenging subject to students with such diverse ability levels. She started the year using materials from her college chemistry courses and later signed up to serve as a pilot classroom for a conceptually oriented chemistry curriculum because she was provided with a complete set of teaching materials. Nevertheless, Tara found herself taking work home almost every night for what she described as a "twenty-four-hour-a-day job." Tara explained:

> When I take work home, which I usually do, my goal is to either grade assignments or to read over at least two from each class. I get a feel for where I need to take the next day's lesson. I know how well I'm teaching, if it's coming across. So about 8:00 I start school work, and on a day where I'm really psyched, I can be up to like one or two in the morning.

Lacking the time she desired with her own children, Tara felt pulled between the needs of her students and those of her family.

In addition to feeling pressed for time, Tara was also frustrated with the lack of resources at her school, and the absence of a science laboratory in particular. Although promised a fully equipped laboratory when hired, this classroom space was not completed until March, and even at that point undersupplied. Tara explained:

> When I was hired, I was told that the lab would be complete and that would be my classroom. So, back in September I was told, in two weeks be prepared to move your class over completely into the lab. And I was psyched, [my students] were psyched, and we were like, two weeks and we're outta here. This is only a temporary space, and then we can do real labs.

She had moved from a pharmaceutical context where she could spend $1,500 a day on supplies to a teaching context where "I have to take everything home, I dishwash everything, and then I bring it back." Even when the lab was eventually ready, it was still short safety items like coats, goggles, and gloves; used borrowed glassware from an adjoining middle school; and was missing many items necessary for her curriculum. Nevertheless, Tara was excited to finally get her students into a laboratory context where she could begin to share her expertise on lab protocol. She commented, "Getting them into the lab and doing hands-on activities is so much more valuable for quite a number of the students than giving them a reading." Although Tara and her students enjoyed using the lab throughout the spring, at the end of the school year Tara learned that her school would be relocated the following year and she would lose this laboratory space she had worked so hard to create.

Leaving Unexpectedly

Frustrated with the loss of her lab and a general lack of consistency among her school's administration, Tara nevertheless prepared to return to teaching the following year and focus on readying her students for the state's biology exit exam. She said, "I think about the other teachers I know who are in their first year and ready to quit. Being through challenges makes you stronger." At times, Tara felt that she was in a burnout profession and that the school's chaotic context hid her struggles as a teacher. She commented, "In some respects, I don't feel like I'm being developed. I'm just pretty much testing new approaches out on these kids, and there's no support there for me to say, okay, you really don't want to do that."

Despite these challenges, Tara planned to return to teaching, pursue her teaching certificate, and help raise student test scores. However, during a midsummer professional development workshop, Tara learned about a job opportunity on a mobile educational lab, where she could travel the state, bringing high-tech laboratory experiences to students.

She was encouraged to apply, and after seeing the higher salary and benefits, Tara accepted the job in late August, just before the start of the next school year. In addition to returning to close to her pharmaceutical salary, she also reasoned, "In six years I'll be forty, and I don't want to be a teacher when I'm forty. I don't want to say that I'm a teacher when I turn forty." While remaining within the field of education, Tara moved into a nonclassroom role after one year of full-time teaching.

Exploring, Again

Tara worked at the mobile educational lab for three years and was generally pleased with the position. For one, the shortened workweek offered her more time with her children: "It's especially nice to be able to go into my son's school and help with his homework." She also felt that the students she worked with were generally engaged and motived to learn the materials and that the job was less stressful. Tara explained, "I don't feel stressed at all working in this program. I think my stress in teaching came from feeling as though I was responsible for fifty students and what they learned. In this program, I feel like that stress isn't there. So the key thing is having them understand how basic science works."

Moreover, her planning and preparation responsibilities went down considerably, as "once one lab is done maybe two or three times, you get a feel for it, and it's not like 'oh, I have to go home and study it' because it just flows." Despite her satisfaction with her current position, Tara knew from the start that this was not a long-term profession and continually played with other career options, including the recurring dream of medicine, noting, "I'd really like to have a doctor attached to my name."

After three years at the mobile educational laboratory, where she enjoyed her work but felt that the constant travel around the state was taking its toll, Tara decided, "This isn't something I can retire out of." She had just had her third child and said, "I didn't see myself, in my forties, trooping around the state teaching." While she yearned to get back in the lab, saying, "I missed research. I missed doing DNA work, I knew that much," she did not want to return to the disconnected work of pharmaceutical research, where "depending on the direction the research project went, it could be tossed overnight or might go to market twenty years later."

Inspired by popular television shows and a forensics lab she developed for students during her time at the mobile educational lab, Tara decided to make a career change into forensic science. She explained her reasoning: "While I was [developing the lab], it kind of piqued my interest too so I was like, 'Oh, this is something I could do. It sounds like it's interesting and it would always be relevant as long as there was crime.'" After two initial rejection letters from local forensic labs, Tara learned that despite her master's degree in biology and her years of DNA lab experience, she still needed additional training in order to secure a position in this competitive field. She enrolled in a second bachelor's degree program in forensic studies, where she attended night classes for a year.

Settling on a New Career Path

After completing her training, Tara was hired as a forensic analyst for a local police department. In this role, she tested DNA evidence, wrote reports, and testified about her findings in court. Tara was pleased with her new job and the way that it helped crime victims, suspects, and their families. Moreover, her new job was never boring: "Even though types of crime are the same, the stories are different. So it doesn't get boring because, say, I'm looking for blood all the time, that's routine. But it's the story of why I'm looking for blood for a particular case—or any other body fluid—that makes it more interesting." While Tara at times feels pressured to focus on high-profile cases and preferred to simply work on one case at a time, overall she enjoyed her new career and could see herself there for a long time. Plus she enjoyed "being in the know" about crime in her region.

Although there was not much room for advancement in her position, as lab managers primarily do unappealing grant writing, Tara was happy to work as a forensic analyst for years to come. She noted, "I can see myself doing this twenty years down the road. I'm really happy that this turned out to be what I expected and more." In fact, she saw it as a real career, noting:

> I think this is more of a career. William City Pride initially, I thought, maybe could have been a career. I was looking for a career change; I thought teaching could have been it. And then I was just like, "No. Not this way."

Once she settled into her new career, Tara and her husband bought a home in the area on six acres of land. While Tara still worked long hours, she also had the time to spend with her three children after work was over for the day.

Despite her career change out of the field of education, Tara continued to use her teaching skills as an adjunct instructor in her former forensic studies program. In this role, she maintained a connection to her years of teaching. Plus she had a lot to offer her students in terms of teaching them both lab protocol and firsthand practical experience. Tara explained the job hunting process for forensic analysts, warning her students, "Prepare to be waiting a year or two years before you hear anything and that's normal." She also emphasized lab protocol because this was the first lab experience for some of her students.

From her years of teaching, Tara learned "not to assume that they know," and instead reminded students to use their lab notebooks to refresh themselves on important techniques. Tara said, "I'm doing what I really enjoy and having that personal growth, but then sharing what I learn with students who are trying to come into the field." She characterized that as "the best of both worlds." Her seven-year career trajectory took her from teaching into an education-related field and finally out of education altogether.

THEMES

Despite individual pathways, some important parallels emerged for the three case study teachers who transitioned out of the field of education. Together, their experiences illustrate the high costs of conceptualizing of teaching as an exploratory career and the challenges of transitioning out of education and into another field. However, they also highlight the ways in which these three teachers continue to use their instructional skills for the benefit of others.

Theme #1: Leavers Saw Teaching as Temporary

These three former teachers all entered education with the intent of exploring it as a potential profession. None of them initially envisioned themselves as career educators and none secured formal teacher preparation prior to entering the classroom. Alexandra applied to Teach for America in her senior year of college because she saw it as a way to delay the process of figuring out exactly what she wanted to do with her life. Likewise, Charlotte entered teaching as an explicitly transitional period between two graduate programs. While she opened herself up to the possibility that she might love teaching enough that she wanted to stay, she intended to teach only for the short term. Finally, Tara also entered teaching with the idea that it might constitute a more family-friendly profession than pharmaceutical research. She also was open to the idea that this might offer a new career path for her, but was disappointed in several ways with what she found in the urban schools.

In addition to entering teaching with the intention of exploring it as a potential career, these three individuals also decided within their first few years in the classroom that education was not going to become their lasting profession. Here the decision-making process appeared to contain two phases. First, these educators decided that teaching did not constitute the career they had envisioned for themselves. Alexandra decided that another field would better fit her goal of translating science to the public, Charlotte wanted to draw upon her scientific knowledge and training in a more explicit way, and Tara wanted to use her laboratory skills while also striking a reasonable work-life balance. Moreover, all three teachers felt exhausted and stressed by their work, with both Alexandra and Charlotte taking several months off afterward to emotionally and physically recover. Their initial decisions that teaching would constitute a short-term occupation appeared to emerge out of their intentions and professional goals, rather than some specific workplace situation.

After making the decision that teaching was a short-term endeavor, these educators then waited until the workplace conditions were right before they initiated a change. Alexandra made her move after a change in the school's administration that left her in a far more marginal role as internship and technology coordinator. Charlotte left after a significant downturn in the school's climate and the departure of many of her colleagues. And Tara left when she was essentially recruited for a position with higher salary and benefits. While negative workplace conditions and/or positive career opportunities seemed to enable the career moves, they did not appear to be the primary motivators for change. Rather, Alexandra, Charlotte, and Tara had already been considering their professional opportunities for some time and planning alternative career trajectories.

Theme #2: Leaving Proved an Extended and Difficult Process

After leaving the classroom, all three of these former teachers entered into an extended and at times difficult transitional period. As mentioned above, both Alexandra and Charlotte took several months off to travel, sleep, exercise, read books, and generally take care of themselves. Moreover, all three of these teachers found that they needed considerable retraining in order to be able to move out of education. At the time that she left the schools, Alexandra had already for several years pursued advanced training in the field of public health, earning a master's degree in public health through online and summer courses. Tara also returned to school, earning a second bachelor's degree in forensic science.

For both Alexandra and Tara, this continued training must have come at great personal cost, because the coursework was completed on top of a full-time job and, for Tara, also raising three young children. While Charlotte did not ultimately return to school, she did endure over a year in what she considered an unpleasant administrative position because she thought it would offer her the time and ability to take more classes. In addition to the advanced education and retraining, all three former teachers spent an extended period of time searching for new positions, received numerous rejection letters, and even were forced to accept jobs below their educational and skill levels in order to make ends meet.

Theme #3: Leavers Retained Some Lasting Connection to Education

Although the experiences of these three women highlight the difficulties of exploring teaching as a profession as well as the costs of transitioning out of education, they also demonstrate the strong connection that remains even after teachers have left the field. All three of these former teachers continued to retain some link to the field of education and use their instructional skills in diverse ways. Alexandra, for instance, envisioned her new career in public health as an extension of her work in the science classroom. For her, educating the public was simply a larger-scale version of educating her students about the findings and applications of science.

Moreover, she used her knowledge of the school system daily in administrative work at the school district office. Charlotte worked numerous part-time jobs in science education as an adjunct instructor, professional developer, and curriculum evaluator. While she no longer saw herself as an educator, she enjoyed the work of mentoring practicing teachers and facilitating their creative use of the science content. And Tara used her educational skills as an adjunct instructor in her former forensic science program. She was explicit about using what she learned from her time in the classroom to support her current students, including building upon their prior knowledge and using formative assessment techniques. Although no longer in formal teaching positions as part of the K–12 school system, these educators nonetheless brought their curriculum, instruction, and assessment skills into society at large, provided enhanced educational opportunities for those they came into contact with, and maintained their connection to the field in enduring ways.

SIX

Listening to Teachers

The teaching profession today operates under old norms within a new social context. Today's teachers have far more professional opportunities available to them in the workplace (Johnson, 2004), they envision multi-dimensional and dynamic career pathways (Dwyer & Wyn, 2001), and they find a menu of teacher preparation options (Zeichner & Conklin, 2005). Some new teachers, across a range of classroom settings, continue to come to education with the goal of pursuing it as a longstanding future career. They find a variety of both traditional and alternative pathways to facilitate their entry into the classroom. And they work within structures that assume a thirty-year career in classroom teaching. For those who come to education with the goal of remaining in the field over the long term, these structures support their development as professionals over time.

However, there is a growing consensus in the research literature (e.g., Freedman & Applebaum, 2008; Peske, Liu, Johnson, Kauffman, & Kardos, 2001; Smethem, 2007; Watt et al., 2012) that others operating within the current exploratory context see their time in the classroom as more of a temporary stop along a much longer and more multifaceted professional journey. These teachers find their routes into the classroom eased by alternative certification, but once they are in the classroom operate within the same structures as their more linear counterparts. They also imagine that their routes out of the classroom and into their desired fields will mirror their transition in; but they encounter unanticipated obstacles along the way, largely stemming from the low exchange value of the field of education (Maier, 2012).

The present study finds that teachers themselves can articulate how they envision their future professional pathways as early as the first few years in the classroom. Some teachers see themselves as educational professionals and mediate their career choices through this lens, choosing to navigate workplace challenges or shift into education-related roles while remaining committed to the larger field. Others, however, see themselves as experimenting with teaching and use their time in the classroom to inform their next career steps. There is no evidence to indicate these two groups of teachers differ in their pedagogical effectiveness or day-to-day commitment to students. Their primary distinction lies in the way that they envision and construct their career pathways, with one group choosing to remain in the field of education in varying roles and capacities, while the other elects to leave for other fields when teaching no longer meets their personal or professional needs.

This research also finds that teachers' original intentions to either remain in or move out of the field of education mediate their experiences in schools over time, such that their intentions serve as guiding lenses for interpreting the workplace. In this way we see that in today's exploratory environment, teachers not only draw upon their intentions at the initiation of their careers but also time and time again as they move through their careers. Teachers' intentions with respect to the educational systems serve as unspoken actors shaping their reaction to school-based rewards and challenges, guiding them to alternately stay in the classroom, shift to education-related roles, or leave education altogether.

Despite evidence that today's teachers are divided in how they see their careers in the classroom, the structures of teacher recruitment, support, and retention have remained essentially unchanged in the face of this new exploratory context. While teachers today come to the classroom with varying visions and plans for their own professional growth, the teaching profession rarely attends to these perspectives, despite their critical influence in shaping career trajectories. Multiple routes into the classroom have expanded in recent decades, but even within these preparation pathways teachers' perspectives are rarely accounted for. Prospective teachers' test scores, academic achievement, dispositions, and leadership skills are evaluated, but these cannot provide a window into their perspectives on the profession. Once in the classroom, schools attend to working conditions, leadership, autonomy, and support, all ingredients for a well-functioning school. But again, these features fail to shed light or draw upon teachers' lenses on the profession.

With teachers able to accurately identify and articulate their professional plans so early, it seems essential that the teaching profession pay close attention to what they have to say. While schools and school districts, in urban and other low-income areas in particular, struggle with teacher recruitment and retention, they overlook a valuable source of information on teachers' career pathways: the teachers themselves. This research suggests that it is critical for teacher preparation programs, school districts, and school leaders to attend more closely to teachers' intentions in the field of education in order to understand and ultimately cater to the professional needs of all educators in today's exploratory professional context. By attending more closely to the perspectives teachers bring to the profession and the plans that shape their career directions over time, the teaching profession may be able to adjust its norms to better suit the new social context.

LISTENING AS A WAY TO VALUE TEACHERS

Many countries around the world struggle with similar challenges of recruiting and retaining a teaching workforce; however, these issues are curiously not universal. According to a recent OECD report (2005), countries that hold teachers in high regard have larger numbers of qualified teaching applicants and far lower rates of teacher attrition than their counterparts. One element of this situation can most certainly be attributed to public perceptions of teaching. We know that Singapore, for instance, had both raised salaries so that they are equivalent to other professions and also emphasized the contribution of teachers in the public image (Goodwin, 2012). Likewise, in Finland, teachers are not paid at substantially higher rates than in other countries, but they are viewed as central to Finnish society and are considered among the most admired professionals (Sahlberg, 2010). Both of these countries face few challenges with teacher recruitment and retention.

For countries like Singapore and Finland, where many qualified candidates compete for top spots in teacher preparation programs, the process of entry into teaching already incorporates close attention to teachers' perceptions of the field and professional plans. In Singapore, for instance, qualified teaching applicants are interviewed and questioned about their "interest in teaching, goals, and aspirations" (Goodwin, 2012, p. 28). Likewise, in Finland teaching applicants must pass a national entrance exam containing questions on wide-ranging educational issues as well as complete an interview where they are asked to explain why they would like to become teachers (Sahlberg, 2010). These responses are taken into consideration as part of a highly competitive selection process.

Countries like Singapore and Finland, which not only hold teachers in high regard but also attain top student achievement scores on international exams, have already begun listening to teachers' ideas and plans even before they enter the profession. If the United States and other countries that continue struggling to strengthen and solidify their teacher workforce can learn from successful international models, they may begin raising the status of teachers and attending to teachers' perspectives for the benefit of all. We know that salary is one key element in profession building, but by no means the only factor in how teaching is valued (Darling-Hammond, 2010). While listening to teachers cannot alone raise the status of the profession, it is certainly one element in offering teachers professional autonomy to construct both their classrooms and their careers in ways that are sensible to them.

HOW TO LISTEN TO TEACHERS

The section that follows highlights the recruitment approaches of three very distinct schools and school districts across the United States. They have been selected because they are attempting to listen in meaningful ways to teachers' ideas and plans as part of their recruitment and development processes and, consequently, respect teachers' ability to conceptualize and construct their own teaching careers. The three schools and school districts selected serve a variety of student populations—from relatively homogeneous and middle class to more diverse and disadvantaged. They operate under different missions, organizational structures, and school cultures. And each has developed a unique approach to recruiting, supporting, and retaining educators who will thrive within their school context.

What cuts across these three examples is that each one, in its own way, takes the time to carefully attend to teachers' ideas about the teaching profession and their role in it as part of the recruitment process. In this way, each school or school district makes careful decisions about who will join their ranks and simultaneously values teachers' input into their own career trajectories. These three examples, which have been drawn from interviews with principals, school leaders, and human resource directors, as well as a review of materials related to recruitment, evaluation, support, and retention, are meant to serve as models by which other schools and districts might begin to incorporate teachers' perspectives and plans into their hiring processes, thereby listening to and respecting teachers right from the start.

Central Penn High School: Maintaining a Tradition of Excellence

Central Penn High School draws students from fifty-six square miles of townships in central Pennsylvania and is considered one of the most academically successful school districts in the region, boasting 88.7 percent of students graduating and 79 percent planning to pursue higher education. Central Penn, which enrolls approximately 1,200 students, has a relatively homogeneous and middle-class student population, with 91.46 percent of the students White and 24 percent qualifying for free and reduced lunch. Central Penn's mission revolves around the importance of community and personal growth, stating that it aims to provide:

> a continually improving educational environment, through a cooperative effort with the family and the entire community, in which all students are encouraged and expected to achieve their full potential, to

express themselves clearly, to think reflectively, and to interact respon-
sibly in preparation for lifelong personal growth. (District website,
2013)

This mission is reflected in their recruitment and hiring practices, which
also prioritize personal and community connections for their teachers.

Mr. William Grant has been the principal of Central Penn High School
for the past ten years and during this time has observed that when rare
openings do come up at the school from among their ninety-six teachers,
there can be anywhere from twenty to fifty or more qualified applications
for each, depending on the field. Not only are openings rare at Central
Penn, but they typically come from retirements, as Mr. Grant can only
recall perhaps three or four teachers over his tenure at the school leaving
for personal reasons such as geographic relocation. In ten years, only one
newly hired teacher has decided to leave the field of education altogether, prior to even starting the school year. This suggests an annual attrition
rate hovering close to 2 percent, far below the national average of approximately 14 percent (Ingersoll & May, 2010), and closer to the 3 percent
reported internationally by countries that hold teachers in high regard,
such as Korea, Italy, and Japan (OECD, 2005).

When Mr. Grant does have an opening at Central Penn, he puts applicants through an extensive and multistage hiring process that includes
getting to know teaching applicants on a personal level to assure that
they will contribute positively to his community of educators, students,
and families. In addition to inspecting their test scores and academic
backgrounds, Mr. Grant also looks to see if they have prior experience
working with children and youth in informal settings. To him, these
camp counselor and youth group positions suggest "that they like being
around kids and they're going to do something whether they get paid or
not." He also likes to see applicants who have tried other fields before
turning to teaching because he sees this as indicating that "they just had
that passion to teach and they could have made a lot more money somewhere else but this is what they wanted to do. That's a really good sign
that they really, really want to be here." Mr. Grant wants applicants who
are committed to students and have demonstrated that they really want
to be teachers.

After reviewing applications, Mr. Grant and his administrative team
bring applicants in for interviews. These interviews are intentionally
structured in an informal manner to help them get to know potential
teachers on a personal level. Mr. Grant explains, "Our goal is to make the
candidates feel comfortable, because then we get the true person. We try
to make it very relaxed so that they really let their true identity shine
through." They also look to see if the applicants feel comfortable talking
about their teaching, their work with students, and their passions within
the field. The first interview is followed by a second interview at the

building level, a third with the district superintendent, reference checks, and finally a job offer. Mr. Grant's own children attend Central Penn; he looks upon every teacher hire as if he or she were responsible for his own family, noting, "Personally, my four kids have either graduated from here or are currently in this school, so if I wouldn't want my own child in the classroom I wouldn't want anybody else's child in the classroom."

In addition to the personal connection so vital to Mr. Grant's hiring approach, Central Penn also emphasizes a community connection. A large number of the teachers hired at Central Penn have graduated from the high school themselves and return to teach there even if they themselves cannot afford to live in the district. While this community connection is by no means a requirement, Mr. Grant particularly likes to hire district graduates because they already understand the commitment required to the school and community and have returned in order to "maintain that tradition of excellence." They recognize that they will be coming in early, staying late, and taking the initiative to work with students above and beyond the formal school day. Mr. Grant notes, "They know the quality of education that the students get and they want to be a part of that. They come, they're hired, and they stay."

Once hired, teachers at Central Penn participate in an induction process and frequent walkthrough observation during the three years until tenure and beyond. Mr. Grant notes that while he wants all teachers to be successful, some are "supervised out" if they are not meeting his expectations with respect to instructional delivery and evidence of student learning. At Central Penn, it is more common for a teacher to be supervised out of the school prior to tenure than to elect to leave the school voluntarily. For those who do stay, though, Mr. Grant describes Central Penn as a family. Teachers also report the same sentiment, saying, "It is like a family. I just love it here. I don't want to leave." And as the sign in the front of the main office notes, "Our school is number one because of its dedicated professionals. They deserve your courtesy and respect."

The Equity Project: Finding the Right Fit

The Equity Project (TEP) Charter School is a middle school that opened in September of 2009 in the Washington Heights neighborhood of New York City, a predominantly Latino and low-income community. TEP has drawn national attention in the news media as an innovative experiment in school reform because of its emphasis on teacher quality and its annual teacher salary of $125,000 (Gootman, 2008, 2009). TEP's model prioritizes sustainability and the school does not fundraise to support teacher salaries, only for the development of a school facility. Instead, it draws upon savings in other areas such as administration and consulting services to support its compensation model. TEP's website encapsulates its three-pronged approach as "Rigorous Qualifications, Redefined Expectations, & Revolutionary Compensation." TEP uses this approach to begin shaping a future where teachers are valued as professionals. TEP's mission captures its goals on three levels:

Teacher Level: TEP aims to reimagine the teaching profession as a place in which teachers prioritize their own growth—as pedagogical experts, content specialists, intellectual seekers, and community leaders.

Student Level: TEP aims to achieve educational equity for students from low-income families by utilizing world-class teachers to maximize every student's academic and personal potential.

Societal Level: TEP aims to inspire others to effect positive systemic change by investing in teacher equity in the form of rigorous qualifications, redefined expectations, and revolutionary compensation.

Through its innovative approach, TEP aims to not only recruit but also support and sustain a corps of master teachers.

Mr. Zeke Vanderhoek is the founder and principal of TEP, where he spearheads teacher recruitment efforts. TEP teachers are hired on annual contracts and must demonstrate strong student achievement in order to return the following year. In the first four years of the school, TEP has averaged an approximately 25 percent attrition rate, primarily due to nonrenewal, although a small minority of teachers has also left to pursue other professional opportunities. Given TEP's compensation model, the school receives numerous applications from experienced and qualified educators across the country for each open position. TEP's rigorous hiring process includes a written application with evidence of student learning and an original curricular tool, a demonstration lesson and interview, and a full day of teaching at the school. Throughout the process, candidates are formally evaluated based on teaching expertise and experience, expert subject-area knowledge, curriculum development ability, and verbal skills.

As part of this formal hiring process, Mr. Vanderhoek also carefully assesses candidates' fit within the larger school culture. He notes that this idea of fit was not initially part of his recruitment process, but rather something that has developed over time as he determined which teachers were the most successful with his school and students. He notes that fit for TEP constitutes a particular combination of qualities, including commitment to the low-income student population, stamina within a high-intensity environment, and openness to participating in a critical culture of feedback. He finds that fit is not always self-evident:

Fit means the ability to participate in a feedback and collaborative-oriented culture. The kind of people we want to attract are the people who are really attracted to growth, have a growth orientation, and want to learn from talented peers. A lot of people think they want that but are not necessarily used to it, especially if they've been a real great teacher at a school where they close their classroom door. So if you're not open to growth in a way that can be uncomfortable, then it's not a great fit.

Also central to TEP's notion of fit are ten staff norms that have been articulated by the school (see table 6.1), including everything from maintaining positivity to communicating effectively with colleagues to respectfully managing time. Through his interactions with teaching candidates, Mr. Vanderhoek looks carefully for fit from multiple perspectives, because, as he notes, "Fit is very hard to teach."

Once hired by TEP, teachers are carefully evaluated on a combination of primary domains: (A) Professional Expectations, (B) Adherence to

Table 6.1.   Staff Norms at TEP

Staff Norms

Norm 1: We will prioritize the needs of the entire school (all students and faculty) over the needs of a particular grade team, department team, whole school service team, classroom, or individual.

Norm 2: We will maintain positivity toward students, staff, and parents by assuming the best intentions, accepting changes made for the good of the school, trusting the process, and remaining adaptable and flexible.

Norm 3: We will dare to have difficult conversations regarding professional matters with an eye on finding solutions. If an issue arises with a coworker, we will go directly to that person FIRST; if the issue remains unresolved, we will get help from the appropriate third party.

Norm 4: We will refrain from gossip and directly address negative talk when we hear it.

Norm 5: We will communicate to and for our teammates any perceived inequity in order to be aware of and promote equity amongst staff, without allowing each other to relinquish our responsibilities.

Norm 6: We will support each other but not allow ourselves to be carried; we will instead seek and offer empowering support.

Norm 7: We will model student behavior norms. This means that we will act honestly, ethically, and respectfully at all times, and follow school rules.

Norm 8: We will present a united front to students (e.g., coteaching, discipline).

Norm 9: We will respect colleagues' time by beginning and ending classes and meetings on time, observing planning time protocols, and reporting for duties on time; we will also communicate and document individual boundaries within grade level teams/departments.

Norm 10: We will all be cognizant that we are "works in progress" and will give and receive feedback in an open, honest, and respectful manner; we will also admit mistakes and apologize as appropriate.

TEP's Staff Norms, (C) Classroom Management, (D) Instructional Planning and Delivery, and (E) Assessment of Student Growth, as well as Secondary Domains: (A) Teacher Partnerships, (B) Whole School Service, (C) Extended-Day Activities, (D) Hallway Transitions, (E) Physical Classroom Environment, and (F) Administrative Responsibilities. While administrators hold primary responsibility for teacher evaluation and retention decisions, other constituencies such as students and colleagues are also included as part of the process. Notably, teachers' fit within the school culture continues to be assessed through peer evaluation of the ten staff norms.

Finally, Mr. Vanderhoek argues that, just as he expects his teachers to continually learn and grow, so he continually refines his practices. His hiring process is dynamic and responsive to an evolving notion of fit within the school culture. He explains:

> The main thing is that it's not static. I'm telling you what we've learned over the past four years, and I'm sure we'll learn just as much in the next four. I'm not sure [what the future will bring], but I know we're continually refining what we want and what works.

It seems that Mr. Vanderhoek fits right in with the TEP school culture.

Aspire Public Schools: Developing Expertise

Aspire Public Schools is a network of thirty-four charter schools serving low-income communities across the state of California. Aspire's student population is 70 percent low income and 80 percent minority. Aspire has received international attention for its high academic performance on a large scale as well as its sustained improvement over time (Mourshed, Chijioke, & Barber, 2010). According to the network's website, the twelve thousand students served by Aspire significantly outperform not only other low-income communities but also the state of California as a whole based on the state's Academic Performance Index, a compilation of academic measures. Aspire's mission centers on what they term a "College for Certain" culture that makes a college education "the expectation—not the exception" for students who would not typically receive college preparation. Aspire has been tremendously successful in reaching this goal. Since its founding, Aspire has maintained a 95 percent graduation rate, a 99 percent college acceptance rate, and an 87 percent college persistence rate.

Dr. Heather Kirkpatrick leads Aspire in the role of "Chief People Officer," which includes responsibilities for both human resources and education. With a fairly typical teacher attrition rate of approximately 20 percent, Dr. Kirkpatrick is involved in recruiting new educators for Aspire's teacher residency program. This program enrolls approximately thirty residents per year who spend four days a week in a mentor teacher's classroom as well as one day each week completing coursework. At the conclusion of a year, teacher residents earn a teaching certificate, a master's degree, and a small stipend. As Dr. Kirkpatrick notes, they are also "practically guaranteed a job at one of our schools." In addition to the teacher residency program, teachers may also be directly recruited to school sites at Aspire, where school principals have the autonomy to make their own hiring decisions.

Dr. Kirkpatrick describes the culture at Aspire as one in which teachers are supported as they intentionally develop their expertise over time. She notes:

> One of the pushes in the organization is to create an opportunity for teachers who really do want to teach for thirty years, who are incredibly committed to the notion of practice makes perfect, the ten thousand hours, twenty thousand hours, thirty thousand hours of deliberate practice. We want experts and we don't think you can get to expertise without years and years and years of trying hard and coming back again and reflecting and refining.

Their recruitment practices in the residency mirror this culture with a strong focus on passion for and commitment to teaching. Dr. Kirkpatrick explains, "What we are really hiring you for is a love of teaching. We are looking for people who want to do this for the rest of their lives."

Like Mr. Vanderhoek's notion of fit, Dr. Kirkpatrick and her team also use a variety of measures to assess candidates' level of commitment to the profession right from the start. The written application to Aspire's residency program includes a four-part statement of purpose that explicitly directs candidates to discuss their purposefulness and commitment to teaching as a lifelong profession, along with ownership and customer service (see Statement of Purpose guidelines in table 6.2). Teaching residency candidates are also interviewed for the program, where the questions change from year to year but again attempt to pull out these same notions of purposefulness and commitment. Dr. Kirkpatrick notes that during the application and interview process, many of the most successful candidates will indicate that they have wanted to be a teacher their whole lives.

Another piece of Aspire's culture that Dr. Kirkpatrick and her team emphasize up front is how difficult the work of a teacher can be, particularly in low-income communities. They try to make the challenges explicit so that future educators come into the field aware of and ready for the obstacles that lie ahead. Dr. Kirkpatrick notes:

> We're really looking for people who can tell us a story of being okay with things being hard and being organized enough to get through the millions of demands that are made on you as a teacher and as a resident.

Table 6.2. Aspire Teacher Residency Statement of Purpose

Statement of Purpose

Section 1 (Purposefulness and Commitment to Teaching as a Lifelong Profession)
Please tell us your story, describing your professional, educational, and personal path towards deciding to become a teacher in an urban school system. What successes and obstacles have you overcome to get to this place?

Section 2 (Purposefulness and Commitment to Teaching as a Lifelong Profession)
Tell us why you plan on spending four or more years of your life as a teacher with Aspire Public Schools. Please include prior experiences working with children.

Section 3 (Ownership)
Describe the job or task where you have been least effective. What do you think the reasons are? What did you do to address the difficulty of the job and improve your work?

Section 4 (Customer Service)
Describe experiences you have had in which you had to relate to people/cultures/ experiences different from your own. Describe what you learned about yourself as a result of these experiences AND what makes you believe that you will be able to serve all Aspire students.

While reviewing applications, Aspire Teacher Residency looks at eight specific competencies including: purposefulness, ownership, collaboration, customer service, quality, perseverance, communication, and a commitment to teaching as a lifelong profession.

They also look for what Dr. Kirkpatrick calls a "sense of urgency" about the importance of preparing young people for "the future." She explains that at Aspire:

> There is a real sense of urgency. I believe that to be a great teacher you should have that sense of urgency no matter who you're serving. I feel like rich, poor, Brown, Black, White, I don't care. You have a really limited amount of time with these kids. If you want to be a knockout teacher you've got to use that time wisely.

Dr. Kirkpatrick believes that these three qualities, "honoring the profession," "knowing how hard it is and not pretending that it's not that hard," and maintaining a "sense of urgency" characterize the teachers who thrive at Aspire. Her recruitment team actively seeks out like-minded individuals to join their ranks.

Once hired, Aspire teachers hear again and again: "We're trying to create a place you want to be for thirty years as a teacher, where it's exciting and challenging and productive and satisfying." Aspire evaluates its teachers using six different measures from administrator, peer, student, family, and student achievement sources, and identifies five levels of effectiveness based on those measures. As teachers develop in their effectiveness, Aspire also offers a multitude of professional opportunities, the majority of which involve remaining in the classroom, so that they can continue learning and growing. Aspire has structured these professional growth opportunities so that teachers can begin taking them on even in early stages of effectiveness, such that almost all teachers at Aspire have elected some form of additional training or leadership role.

Finally, Dr. Kirkpatrick believes that Aspire stands out because of the extent to which they value the input of their teachers. She reflects:

> I think one of the things that has made us successful to date in all sorts of ways is how much we listen to our teachers. And not only do we solicit [feedback], but we pore over the answers. Every survey I open, my stomach hurts, because I'm terrified. They are brutally honest. But the beautiful thing is we've made lots and lots of changes based on the feedback and we have gotten better.

At Aspire, teachers' voices are valued from day one.

Practices for Listening to Teachers

Central Penn, TEP, and Aspire each take their own individual approach to recruiting, supporting, evaluating, and retaining a corps of professional educators. Central Penn favors a natural interview style, TEP emphasizes the process of feedback and refinement, and Aspire closely examines personal stories. What cuts across their approaches is the genuine goal of getting to know their teaching candidates personally and carefully attending not only to their pedagogical skills but also their intentions in the field of education. In addition to taking the time to listen to their applicants, another common thread is a clearly articulated school culture that defines what constitutes a successful professional. These explicit school norms often go hand-in-hand with a well-defined evaluation procedure. With a clear mission that captures the school culture and an explicit articulation of what it takes to be a successful teacher in this environment, all of these school leaders are then able to assess a match between individual teaching candidates and their school, enhancing the quality of teacher recruitment at their school site and valuing teachers' unique ability to provide input into that process.

It is also important to note that each of these three models conceives of teachers as professionals who remain in the classroom over the long term but are not by any means static in their practice. Rather, all three consider teachers to be successful when they learn and grow over time. While that development may take different forms—at Central Penn teachers sponsor extracurricular groups, at TEP they conduct shared inquiries, and at Aspire they take on mentorship or other leadership roles—each school leader recognizes that teachers must be offered opportunities to continually collaborate and refine their practice over time. This suggests that recruitment is not something that ends at the point of hiring, but must be conceptualized in an ongoing manner. Hammerness (2006) describes teaching as a choice that is made again and again and again over the course of a career. Likewise, it seems that recruitment and retention go hand-in-hand as processes that take place again and again and again over the course of educators' careers so that they remain stimulated, productive, and satisfied.

DEVELOPING QUALITY RECRUITMENT

In their VITAE study, Day et al. (2007) argue that the issue of teacher retention should not be framed around the goal of retaining as many teachers as possible. Rather, teacher retention should aim to retain those teachers who maintain their enthusiasm and investment in the career over time. They term this approach "quality retention" and argue:

> Our research suggests the need to distinguish between two forms of retention in the teaching profession: their physical continuation in the role; and the maintenance of motivation and commitment as key indicates of the retention of quality. While the answer to this second form of retention is less easily observed, being located essentially in teachers' values and resilience to meet the challenges of different scenarios in their work and lives, it has major implications for their effectiveness and well-being and for school improvement. We call this second aspect of retention "quality retention." Underlying resilient teachers' endeavours to exert control over difficult situations, is their strength and determination to fulfill their original call to teach, and to manage and thrive professionally. (Day et al., 2007, p. 213)

In this version of teacher retention, continuation in the career is linked not only to effective instruction, but also to teachers' ideas about the profession and their commitment to it.

This research suggests that in order to achieve this goal of quality retention, the teaching profession should likewise adopt the practice of quality recruitment. Just as quality retention aims to ascertain teachers' motivation, commitment, and values with respect to the teaching profession, quality recruitment would enhance the recruitment process by taking into account teachers' views on the teaching profession upon entering the field. Quality recruitment is not meant to suggest raising the quality of the educators themselves, but rather strengthening the recruitment process by attending more carefully to teachers' intentions within the field and drawing upon those intentions as teachers develop their careers over time.

Currently, teacher certification candidates routinely examine their values and beliefs about students, subject matter, teaching, and learning. For instance, National Council for Accreditation of Teacher Education

(NCATE) standards include "Standard 1: Candidates preparing to work in schools as teachers or other school professionals know and demonstrate the content knowledge, pedagogical content knowledge and skills, pedagogical and professional knowledge and skills, and professional dispositions necessary to help all students" (2008). The dispositions assessed in particular focus around notions of fairness and a belief that all students can learn. It seems a logical extension that teaching candidates and teachers might also reflect on their values and beliefs about the teaching profession.

Given the longstanding and influential nature of these views as well as their potential impact upon teacher retention and, in turn, student achievement, it is vital to ask preservice and beginning teachers to articulate their views on the profession as well as their plans within it. This inquiry into views on the profession might take a variety of forms, from personal statements on teacher education applications to collaborative inquiries in coursework to interview questions as part of the hiring process. Whatever the nature of the inquiry, attending to teachers' views on the teaching profession should be a central element for those beginning in the field and should continue in different forms across the professional life span.

Hargreaves and Fullan (2012) highlight the importance of building professional capital among the teacher corps, including human, social, and decisional capital, as a key means for strengthening teaching and learning. As a means to that end, other high-status professions regularly engage in both self-directed and collaborative goal-setting practices that merge professionals' own visions with the directions of the larger organization (Odden, 2011). One way of enhancing the professionalism of teachers in today's exploratory world would be to, in an ongoing manner, engage in goal-setting practices that offer teachers the autonomy to explicitly conceptualize and then direct their own professional pathways. Teacher preparation programs and district and school leaders might facilitate dialogue with teachers about their careers using the sample prompts outlined in table 6.3. These conversations may serve to make teachers' intentions explicit while simultaneously building professional capital and teacher autonomy along their career pathways.

One danger of this approach is that views on the teaching profession might be interpreted in a technical or simplistic manner such that prospective teachers with long-term views would be accepted and short-term views rejected. Or, teachers who pursue more extended preparation routes might be considered more committed than those who pursue abbreviated preparation pathways. This is overly deterministic and not the intended approach. Rather, an articulation of views on the profession should be pursued as an inquiry aimed to clarify and inform the individual far more than as an evaluative measure.

Table 6.3.   Suggested Prompts for Co-constructing Teacher Career Trajectories

Suggested Prompts for Initial Teacher Recruitment

What past experiences in your life motivated you to teach? When you envision your career, what do you see?

How do you typically handle challenges that arise? What are the strengths and weaknesses of that approach?

What concrete steps can you take to build positive relationships with students, colleagues, and school leaders?

What supports will you need in order to be successful? What steps will you take to assure you receive the support you need?

What do you want to focus on during the first year in the classroom? Five years? Ten years?

Suggested Prompts for Beginning Teachers

What have been your greatest successes in the classroom so far? Most difficult challenges? What lessons can you learn from these experiences?

What words would you use to describe your relationships with students, colleagues, and school leaders? What concrete steps can you take to strengthen these relationships even further?

What new challenges would you like to take on? What sparked your interest in these areas? What concrete steps will you take and what obstacles must be overcome in these areas?

What have been the most effective supports you have received so far? What additional supports would you need moving forward?

What would you like to accomplish by the end of next year? In five years? Ten years?

Suggested Prompts for Midcareer Teachers

What have been the most satisfying aspects of your career to date? The most persistent problems? How can you build upon these rewards and challenges in the next career stage?

In what ways have you taken on formal or informal leadership roles? In what ways might you continue to lead? What concrete steps will you take to assure this occurs?

What have been your most satisfying professional relationships? How can you build upon the lessons from these relationships to strengthen future relationships?

How will you define success in the next phase of your career? What supports will you need in order to achieve that definition of success?

Suggested Prompts for Veteran Teachers

What are the most important things you have accomplished professionally? How can you build upon these accomplishments in the next career stage?

In what ways have your professional relationships developed over time? What concrete steps can you take to strengthen them moving forward?

What new things would you like to learn in the coming year?

What have been your most important supports to date? How can you continue
seeking out effective supports while also providing supports to others?

Have you achieved your definition of success? What concrete steps can you take to
continue seeking out your version of success?

It is through the process of critical examination and reflection that
teachers come to better understand their chosen fields, just as they might
come to better understand their students or their pedagogy (e.g., Cochran-Smith & Lytle, 1993). Through this process, prospective and practicing teachers may begin to better understand their views, set goals for
their professional futures, and find greater success in reaching those
goals over time. It may also result in greater commitment to the field or
self-selection out of education altogether. Whatever the outcome, the inquiry process should allow teachers to better understand their chosen
field as well as their role in it.

The act of identifying, examining, and expressing views about the
teaching profession and having those views truly listened to can also
indirectly serve to raise the status of the teaching profession. Rather than
pursuing a career path externally dictated by seniority or credits earned,
teachers who have the ongoing opportunity to explore their professional
directions will have greater autonomy in directing those same careers.
Increasingly, schools and school districts offer a menu of leadership opportunities such that educators can continue learning and growing by
shifting into related roles and responsibilities (Darling-Hammond &
Rothman, 2011). Adding in a stronger practice of goal setting and career
self-direction naturally goes hand-in-hand with these expanded career
options. In this iteration of the profession, teachers' career trajectories are
not externally dictated by central office or school administrators, but
rather coconstructed between teachers and educational leaders in a manner that is more consistent with the expectations of today's collaborative
and autonomous workplaces.

CONCLUSIONS

In this current exploratory context, teachers already actively direct their
own careers by "voting with their feet," entering and leaving the field of
education along ever-shifting personal and professional trajectories that
often leave schools and school districts at a loss for how to effectively
build a stable workforce. While workplace conditions contribute to
movement among institutions, teachers' own ideas about the profession
are also highly influential, particularly in shaping movement into and out
of the field as a whole. This longitudinal research finds that teachers are
aware of their intentions in the profession and use these guiding plans to
shape long-term trajectories. The experiences of these teachers also indi-

cate that leaving comes with high costs not only for schools and students, but also for teachers themselves.

Together, this research suggests that rather than maintaining the status quo, where teachers construct their careers independent of the educational system, we should instead legitimize these multidimensional and dynamic approaches to professional careers, reorganize the practices of recruitment and retention, and encourage teachers to identify their plans, set goals, and construct diverse trajectories in collaborative ways. This will involve educational leaders taking the time to attend to teachers' ideas and coconstructing professional pathways that are consistent with these plans. It will also involve respecting teachers' autonomy to direct their own work lives and valuing their contribution as professionals who want to pursue dynamic, productive, and satisfying careers.

In this way, perhaps the field of education can co-opt the notion of teaching as an exploratory career, such that teachers do not temporarily explore their way into and out of education, but rather continually explore their way through a fulfilling lifelong profession.

Appendix: Semistructured Interview Guide

Semistructured Interview Guide

JANUARY 2006: CURRENT PROFESSIONAL LIFE

1. Tell me about your typical day at school.
2. What are your current rewards at work? *(repeated at every interview)*
3. What are your most difficult challenges? *(repeated at every interview)*

FEBRUARY 2006: LIFE HISTORY

1. Tell me about your experience in school as a student (both K-12 and higher education).

   Where did you attend school? What types of schools did you attend?
   Describe your relationships with teachers and other students.
   Describe the teaching and learning you experienced.
   What were your attitudes toward school as a student?
   What were your attitudes toward science?

2. Tell me about your family.

   Whom did you grow up with? Where?
   What are their occupations?
   What were their expectations of you as a professional?

3. Tell me about your images of a teacher.

   Have there been any changes in these images over time? If so, how?

4. How did you come to teach? Tell me about your pathway into the classroom.

MARCH 2006: ORIENTATIONS TOWARD TEACHING

1. What do you see as the most important aspect(s) of your job?

> If you have only a limited amount of time and resources, where do you put your energy?

2. Is the job what you expected?

> Is the job what others expect? (e.g., friends and family)
> Is the job what it should be?

3. Would you recommend any changes?

> If so, what would your ideal job look like?

4. Have your priorities changed over time? If so, how?

5. What advice would you have for a new urban science teacher just starting out?

APRIL 2006: WORKPLACE CONTEXT AND SUPPORT

1. What types of supports are available to you as a new teacher?

> Tell me about your school-based supports available.
> Tell me about teacher preparation, university-based, or other supports.

2. What supports do you use most regularly?

> Which are the most helpful? Explain.
> Which are the least helpful? Explain.
> Do you provide support to others? Explain.

3. What has been the impact of the support?

> To what extent do you feel like you have accomplished your goals this year?
> How do you measure your own achievement as a teacher?
> To what extent has support played a role in accomplishing those goals?

MAY/JUNE 2006: REFLECTING ON THE YEAR

1. What were some of the most memorable moments from this school year?

> What was memorable inside the classroom? Outside the classroom?
> What was memorable about these incidents?

2. In what ways was this school year what you expected?

In what ways was it not what you expected?

3. To what extent have you accomplished your goals this year? Explain.

To what extent have you not accomplished your goals this year? Explain.
What factors contributed to your ability to accomplish those goals?
What are your goals for next year?

4. Have you changed over the course of the year? Personally or professionally?

AUGUST/SEPTEMBER 2006: PREPARING FOR THE NEW YEAR

1. Describe your professional life this year and if it differs from previous year(s).

What are your priorities or goals?
Describe your work inside the classroom (with students, curriculum, etc.).
Describe your professional interactions and relationships outside of the classroom (with colleagues, administrators, professional developers, etc.).
Describe the relationship between your personal and professional lives.

2. To what extent do you feel successful at school so far this year?

How do you recognize success?
To what extent are you recognized for success?

OCTOBER 2006: ORIENTATIONS TOWARD THE EDUCATIONAL SYSTEM

1. People often say that working in an urban educational system can be challenging because of systemic interferences with your ability to do your job. Have you found this to be true? Please explain.

What types of interferences might hinder your ability to do your job?
What do you do when you are faced with frustrations with the system?
Did you anticipate these types of problems when you started as a teacher?

2. Do you believe that the urban educational system needs to be changed? Explain.

What led you to these conclusions?
Whose responsibility is it to change urban education?

3. What is your role as a part of the larger system?

NOVEMBER/DECEMBER 2006: LONG-TERM CAREER PLANS

1. Describe your short-term career plans.

    What are you considering for the next academic year?
    How did you make that decision?

2. Describe your long-term career plans.

    Where do you see yourself in 5 years? 10? 20?
    How did you develop those plans?
    What are the factors that are most important to you?
    Have these plans changed over time? If so, how and why?

3. Describe your ideal professional life.

    What would be your responsibilities? Work context? Relationship to
    home life?

JANUARY–MARCH 2012: FOLLOW-UP

1. Tell me about your current professional position.

    What are your roles and responsibilities?
    Tell me about your workplace context.
    Tell me about your primary rewards and challenges.
    What are your primary goals? What do you hope to accomplish in this
    role?

2. How did you come to this position? Walk me through your career
pathway from 2006 to 2012.

    Explain how you made your decisions along the way.
    What were the major factors influencing your decision?
    Were there alternatives that you considered and rejected? Decision
    points? Explain.

3. How do you think you've grown and/or changed as a professional
since we last spoke?

    (If teaching)
    Have you evolved pedagogically? If so, how?
    Have you evolved in terms of your relationships with students? If so,
    how?

Have you evolved in terms of your relationships with colleagues and administrators? If so, how?

What have been the major influences on your professional development?

(If no longer teaching)

Have you evolved in terms of your work style? If so, how?

Have you evolved in terms of your relationships with colleagues and supervisors? If so, how?

Do you see a lasting legacy of your years of teaching? In what ways might you have been influenced by your time in the classroom?

What have been the major influences on your professional development?

4. Where do you see yourself going professionally in 5 years? 10 years? 20 years?

What factors do you see influencing your decision making?

Would you make any changes to your pathway?

References

100Kin10. (2013). Answering the nation's call. Retrieved May 22, 2013, fromhttp://www.100kin10.org/.

Biklen, S. K. (1995). *School work: Gender and the cultural construction of teaching*. New York: Teachers College Press.

Bobbitt, S. A., Faupel, E., & Burns, S. (1991). *Characteristics of stayers, movers, and leavers: Results from the teacher follow-up survey, 1988–89*. Washington, DC: Office of Educational Research and Improvement.

Boe, E. E., Bobbitt, S. A., Cook, L. H., Whitener, S. D., & Weber, A. L. (1997). Why didst thou go? Predictors of retention, transfer, and attrition of special and general education teachers from a national perspective. *Journal of Special Education, 30*(4), 390–411.

Borman, G. D., & Dowling, N. M. (2008). Teacher attrition and retention: A meta-analytic and narrative review of the research. *Review of Educational Research, 78*(3), 367–409.

Boyd, D., Lankford, H., Loeb, S., & Wyckoff, J. (2005). The draw of home: How teachers' preferences for proximity disadvantage urban schools. *Journal of Policy Analysis and Management, 24*(1), 113–32.

Bryk, A., & Schneider, B. (2003). Trust in schools: A core resource for school reform. *Educational Leadership, 60*(6), 40–44.

Buchanan, J. (2009). Where are they now? Ex-teachers tell their life-work stories. *Issues in Educational Research, 19*(1), 13.

Buckley, J., Schneider, M., & Shang, Y. (2005). Fix it and they might stay: School facility quality and teacher retention in Washington D.C. *Teachers College Record, 107*(5), 1107–23.

Bullough, R. V. (1989). *First-year teacher: A case study*. New York: Teachers College Press.

Carter, K., & Doyle, W. (1996). Personal narrative and life history in learning to teach. In J. Sikula (Ed.), *Handbook of research on teacher education* (2nd ed., pp. 120–42). New York: Macmillan Library Reference.

Cochran-Smith, M., & Lytle, S. (1993). *Inside outside: Teacher research and knowledge*. New York: Teachers College Press.

Darling-Hammond, L. (2010). *The flat world and education: How America's commitment to equity will determine our future*. New York: Teachers College Press.

Darling-Hammond, L., & Rothman, R. (2011). *Teacher and leader effectiveness in high-performing education systems*. Washington, DC: Alliance for Excellent Education and Stanford, CA: Stanford Center for Opportunity Policy in Education.

Day, C., & Gu, Q. (2010). *The new lives of teachers*. New York: Routledge.

Day, C., Sammons, P., Stobart, G., Kington, A., & Gu, Q. (2007). *Teachers matter: Connecting work, lives and effectiveness*. London: Routledge.

DeAngelis, K. J., & Presley, J. B. (2011). Toward a more nuanced understanding of new teacher attrition. *Education and Urban Society, 43*(5), 598–626.

Denzin, N. K., & Lincoln, Y. S. (2011). Paradigms and perspectives in contention. In N. K. Denzin & Y. S. Lincoln (Eds.), *The SAGE handbook of qualitative research* (4th ed., pp. 91–96). Thousand Oaks, CA: SAGE.

Donaldson, M. L., Johnson, S. M., Kirkpatrick, C. L., Marinell, W. H., Steele, J. L., & Szczesiul, S. A. (2008). Angling for access, bartering for change: How second-stage teachers experience differentiated roles in schools. *Teachers College Record, 110*(5), 1088–114.

Dworkin, A. G. (1980). The changing demography of public school teachers: Some implications for faculty turnover in urban areas. *Sociology of Education, 53*, 65–73.

Dwyer, P., & Wyn, J. (2001). *Youth, education, and risk: Facing the future.* New York: RoutledgeFalmer.

Feiman-Nemser, S., & Floden, R. E. (1986). The cultures of teaching. In M. C. Wittrock (Ed.), *Handbook of research on teaching* (3rd ed.). New York: Macmillan Publishing Company.

Foster, M. (1997). *Black teachers on teaching.* New York: The New Press.

Freedman, S. W., & Applebaum, D. (2008). "What else would I be doing?": Teacher identity and teacher retention in urban schools. *Teacher Education Quarterly, 35*(3), 109–26.

Freedman, S. W., & Applebaum, D. (2009). "In it for the long haul": How teacher education can contribute to teacher retention in high-poverty, urban schools. *Journal of Teacher Education, 60*(3), 323–37.

Friedman, T. (2005). *The world is flat: A brief history of the 21st century.* New York: Farrar, Straus, and Giroux.

Goodson, I. F. (1991). Teachers' lives and educational research. In I. F. Goodson & R. Walker (Eds.), *Biography, identity, and schooling: Episodes in education research* (pp. 137–49). Bristol, PA: The Falmer Press.

Goodson, I. F. (1992). Studying teachers' lives: An emergent field of inquiry. In I. F. Goodson (Ed.), *Studying teachers' lives* (pp. 1–17). New York: Teachers College Press.

Goodwin, A. L. (2012). Quality teachers, Singapore style. *Teacher education around the world: Changing policies and practices* (pp. 22–43). New York: Routledge.

Gootman, E. (2008, March 7). At charter school, higher teacher pay. *New York Times.*

Gootman, E. (2009, June 4). Next test: Value of $125,000-a-year teacher. *New York Times.*

Grissmer, D. A., Flanagan, A., Kawata, J., & Williamson, S. (2000). *Improving student achievement: What state NAEP scores tell us.* Arlington, VA: RAND.

Hammerness, K. (2006). *Seeing through teachers' eyes: Professional ideals and classroom practices.* New York: Teachers College Press.

Hammerness, K. (2008). "If you don't know where you are going, any path will do": The role of teachers' visions in teachers' career paths. *New Educator, 4*(1), 1–22.

Hargreaves, A., & Fullan, M. (2012). *Professional capital: Transforming teaching in every school.* New York: Teachers College Press.

Henry, G., Fortner, K., & Bastian, K. (2012). The effects of experience and attrition for novice high-school science and mathematics teachers. *Science, 335*, 1118–21.

Horng, E. L. (2009). Teacher tradeoffs: Disentangling teachers' preferences for working conditions and student demographics. *American Educational Research Journal, 46*(3), 690–717.

Howe, N., & Strauss, W. (2000). *Millennials rising: The next great generation.* New York: Vintage.

Humphrey, D. C., Wechsler, M. E., & Hough, H. J. (2008). Characteristics of effective alternative teacher certification programs. *Teachers College Record, 110*(1), 1–63.

Imazeki, J. (2002). Teacher attrition and mobility in urban districts: Evidence from Wisconsin. In C. Roellke & J. K. Rice (Eds.), *Fiscal policy in urban education* (pp. 119–36). Greenwich, CT: Information Age Publishers.

Ingersoll, R. M. (1999). The problem of underqualified teachers in American secondary schools. *Educational Researcher, 28*(2), 26–37.

Ingersoll, R. M. (2001). *Teacher turnover, teacher shortages, and the organization of schools.* Seattle, WA: Center for the Study of Teaching and Policy.

Ingersoll, R. M. (2003a). Is there really a teacher shortage? University of Washington: Center for the Study of Teaching and Policy.

Ingersoll, R. M. (2003b). Turnover and shortages among science and mathematics teachers in the United States. In J. Rhoton & P. Bowers (Eds.), *Science teacher retention: Mentoring and renewal* (pp. 1–12). Arlington, VA: National Science Education Leadership Association and National Science Teachers Association Press.

Ingersoll, R. M., & May, H. (2010). The magnitudes, destinations, and determinants of mathematics and science teacher turnover: CPRE Research Report.

Ingersoll, R. M., & Merrill, L. (2012). *Seven trends: The transformation of the teaching force.* Paper presented at the annual meeting of the American Educational Research Association, Vancouver, Canada.

Ingersoll, R. M., & Perda, D. (2011). Is the supply of mathematics and science teachers sufficient? *American Educational Research Journal, 47*(3), 563–94.

Jensen, B., Sandoval-Hernandez, A., Knoll, S., & Gonzalez, E. J. (2012). *The experience of new teachers: Results from TALIS 2008.* Paris, France: OECD Publishers.

Johnson, S. M. (2004). *Finders and keepers: Helping new teachers survive and thrive in our schools.* San Francisco: Jossey-Bass.

Johnson, S. M., Berg, J. H., & Donaldson, M. (2005). *Who stays in teaching and why: A review of the literature on teacher retention.* Cambridge, MA: Harvard Graduate School of Education.

Johnson, S. M., & Birkeland, S. E. (2003). Pursuing a "sense of success": New teachers explain their career decisions. *American Educational Research Journal, 40*(3), 581–617.

Johnson, S. M., Kraft, M. A., & Papay, J. P. (2012). How context matters in high-need schools: The effects of teachers' working conditions on their professional satisfaction and their students' achievement. *Teachers College Record, 114*(10), 1–39.

Ladd, H. (2011). Teachers' perceptions of their working conditions: How predictive of planned and actual teacher movement? *Educational Evaluation and Policy Analysis, 33*(2), 235–61.

Lankford, H., Loeb, S., & Wyckoff, J. (2002). Teacher sorting and the plight of urban schools: A descriptive analysis. *Educational Evaluation and Policy Analysis, 24*(1), 37–62.

Levin, B. B. (2003). *Case studies of teacher development: An in-depth look at how thinking about pedagogy develops over time.* Mahwah, NJ: Lawrence Erlbaum.

Lortie, D. C. (1975). *Schoolteacher: A sociological study.* Chicago: University of Chicago Press.

Maier, A. (2012). Doing good and doing well: Credentialism and Teach for America. *Journal of Teacher Education, 61*(1), 10–22.

Margolis, J. (2008). What will keep today's teachers teaching? Looking for a hook as a new career cycle emerges. *Teachers College Record, 110*(1), 160–94.

Merriam, S. B. (1998). *Qualitative research and case study applications in education.* San Francisco: Jossey-Bass.

Miles, M. B., & Huberman, A. M. (1994). *Qualitative data analysis: An expanded sourcebook* (2nd ed.). Thousand Oaks, CA: Sage Publications.

Moe, A., Pazzaglia, F., & Ronconi, L. (2010). When being able is not enough. The combined value of positive affect and self-efficacy for job satisfaction in teaching. *Teaching and Teacher Education, 26*(5), 1145–53.

Mourshed, M., Chijioke, C., & Barber, M. (2010). *How the world's most improved school systems keep getting better.* London: McKinsey & Company.

Murnane, R. J., & Olsen, R. J. (1990). The effects of salaries and opportunity costs on length of stay in teaching—evidence from North Carolina. *Journal of Human Resources, 25*(1), 106–24.

National Council for Accreditation of Teacher Education. (2008). *Professional standards for the accreditation of teacher preparation institutions.* Washington, DC: National Council for Accreditation of Teacher Education.

NCES. (2008). *Public school teacher, BIE school teacher, and private school teacher data files.* Washington, DC: U.S. Department of Education, National Center for Educational Statistics, Schools and Staffing Survey (SASS).

NCTAF. (2007). Policy brief: The high cost of teacher turnover. Washington, DC: NCTAF.

Ng, J. C., & Peter, L. (2010). Should I stay or should I go? Examining the career choices of alternatively licensed teachers in urban schools. *Urban Review, 42*(2), 123–42.

Nieto, S. (2001). What keeps teachers going? And other thoughts on the future of public education. *Equity & Excellence in Education, 34*(1), 6–15.

Odden, A. (2011). Manage "human capital" strategically. *Phi Delta Kappa, 92*(7), 8–12.

OECD. (2005). *Teachers matter: Attracting, developing, and retaining effective teachers.* Paris, France: OECD Publishing.

OECD. (2009). *Creating effective teaching and learning environments: First results from TALIS.* Paris, France: OECD Publishing

Olsen, B., & Anderson, L. (2007). Courses of action: A report on urban teacher career development. *Urban Education, 42*(1).

Papay, J. P. (2007). *The teaching workforce.* Washington, DC: The Aspen Institute.

Peske, H. G., Liu, E., Johnson, S. M., Kauffman, D., & Kardos, S. M. (2001). The next generation of teachers: Changing conceptions of a career in teaching. *Phi Delta Kappan,* 304–11.

Quartz, K. H., Thomas, A., Anderson, L., Masyn, K., Lyons, K. B., & Olsen, B. (2008). Careers in motion: A longitudinal retention study of role changing among early-career urban educators. *Teachers College Record, 110*(1), 218–50.

Rea, L. M., & Parker, R. A. (2005). *Designing and conducting survey research: A comprehensive guide* (3rd ed.). San Francisco: Jossey-Bass.

Rinke, C. (2009). Finding their way on: Career decision-making processes of urban science teachers. *Science Education, 93*(6), 1096–121.

Rinke, C. (2011). Career trajectories of urban teachers: A continuum of perspectives, participation, and plans shaping retention in the educational system. *Urban Education, 46*(4), 639–62.

Ronfeldt, M., Loeb, S., & Wyckoff, J. (2013). How teacher turnover harms student achievement. *American Educational Research Journal, 50*(1), 4–36.

Rosenholtz, S. J. (1989). *Teachers' workplaces: The social organization of schools.* New York: Longman.

Rosenholtz, S. J., & Simpson, C. (1990). Workplace conditions and the rise and fall of teachers' commitment. *Sociology of Education, 63,* 241–57.

Rots, I., Aelterman, A., Vlerick, P., & Vermeulen, K. (2007). Teacher education, graduates' teaching commitment and entrance into the teaching profession. *Teaching and Teacher Education, 23*(5), 543–56.

Rots, I., Kelchtermans, G., & Aelterman, A. (2012). Learning (not) to become a teacher: A qualitative analysis of the job entrance issue. *Teaching and Teacher Education, 28*(1), 1–10.

Rury, J. (1989). Who became teachers? The social characteristics of teachers in American history. In D. Warren (Ed.), *American teachers: Histories of a profession at work* (pp. 9–48). New York: Macmillan.

Sahlberg, P. (2010). *Finnish lessons: What can the world learn from educational change in Finland?* New York: Teachers College Press.

Schaefer, L. (2013). *Shifting the discourse around early career attrition: From questions of why to questions of how much is at work.* Paper presented at the annual meeting of the American Educational Research Association, San Francisco, CA.

Shen, J. (1998). Alternative certification, minority teachers, and urban education. *Education and Urban Society, 31*(1), 30–41.

Skaalvik, E. M., & Skaalvik, S. (2011). Teacher job satisfaction and motivation to leave the teaching profession: Relations with school context, feeling of belonging, and emotional exhaustion. *Teaching and Teacher Education, 27*(6), 1029–38.

Smethem, L. (2007). Retention and intention in teaching careers: Will the next generation stay? *Teachers and Teaching: Theory and Practice, 13*(5), 465–80.

Smulyan, L. (2004). Choosing to teach: Reflections on gender and social change. *Teachers College Record, 106*(3), 513–43.

Teach for America. (2013). Our mission. Retrieved May 22, 2013, fromhttp://www.teachforamerica.org/our-mission.

The White House. (2013). Educate to innovate. Retrieved May 22, 2013, fromhttp://www.whitehouse.gov/issues/education/k-12/educate-innovate.

Theobald, N. D., & Michael, R. S. (2002). Reducing novice teacher attrition in urban districts: Focusing on the moving target. In C. Roellke & J. K. Rice (Eds.), *Fiscal policy in urban education* (pp. 137–52). Greenwich, CT: Information Age Publishers.

Walker, B. (2008). *Who are the millennials? a.k.a. Generation Y* Detroit, MI: Deloitte Consulting.

Watt, H. M. G., & Richardson, P. W. (2008). Motivations, perceptions, and aspirations concerning teaching as a career for different types of beginning teachers. *Learning and Instruction, 18*(5), 408–28.

Watt, H. M. G., Richardson, P. W., Klusmann, U., Kunter, M., Beyer, B., Trautwein, U., & Baumert, J. (2012). Motivations for choosing teaching as a career: An international comparison using the FIT-Choice Scale. *Teaching and Teacher Education, 28*(6), 791–805.

Yee, S. M.-L. (1990). *Careers in the classroom: When teaching is more than a job.* New York: Teachers College Press.

Yin, R. (2003). *Case study research: Design and methods* (3rd ed.). Thousand Oaks, CA: Sage Publications.

Yonezawa, S., Jones, M., & Singer, N. R. (2011). Teacher resilience in urban schools: The importance of technical knowledge, professional community, and leadership opportunities. *Urban Education, 46*(5), 913–31.

Zeichner, K. M., & Conklin, H. G. (2005). Teacher education programs. In M. Cochran-Smith & K. M. Zeichner (Eds.), *Studying teacher education: The report of the AERA panel on research and teacher education* (pp. 645–736). Mahwah, NJ: Lawrence Erlbaum Associates.

About the Author

Carol R. Rinke is assistant professor at Marist College in Poughkeepsie, New York. A graduate of Stanford University, Teachers College, and the University of Maryland College Park, she taught science and mathematics in urban and suburban schools before pursuing educational research. After her first year in the classroom, she watched eleven out of thirteen colleagues leave, sparking a lifelong interest in teachers' career trajectories. She is the author of over fifteen articles on science teacher career development and teacher education, in journals including *Teachers College Record, Teaching and Teacher Education, Science Education,* and *Urban Education.*